Julie ~ Paul Roberts

C O U N T R Y
Pubs & Inns of
DEVON

By Peter Long

Regional Hidden Places

Cornwall
Devon
Dorset, Hants & Isle of Wight
East Anglia
Gloucs, Wiltshire & Somerset
Heart of England
Hereford, Worcs & Shropshire
Lake District & Cumbria
Lancashire & Cheshire
Northumberland & Durham
Peak District
Sussex
Yorkshire

National Hidden Places

England
Ireland
Scotland
Wales

Hidden Inns

East Anglia
Heart of England
North of England
South
South East
West Country
Yorkshire

Country Pubs & Inns

Cornwall
Devon
Sussex
Wales

Country Living Rural Guides

East Anglia
Heart of England
Ireland
North East of England
North West of England
Scotland
South
South East
Wales
West Country

Published by: Travel Publishing Ltd, 7a Apollo House, Calleva Park, Aldermaston, Berkshire RG7 8TN

ISBN 1-904-43441-X

© Travel Publishing Ltd

Published 2006

Printing by: Scotprint, Haddington

Maps by: © Maps in Minutes ™ (2006)
© Crown Copyright, Ordnance Survey 2006

Editor: Peter Long

Cover Design: Lines and Words, Aldermaston, Berkshire

Cover Photograph: The Castle Inn, Lydford, Devon

Text Photographs: © www.britainonview.com

Foreword

The *Country Pubs & Inns of Devon* is one of a series of guides which will eventually cover the whole of the UK. This guide provides details of pubs and inns (including hotels which welcome non-residents) situated in the countryside of Devon. "Countryside" is officially defined by *The Office of National Statistics* as "settlements of less than 10,000 inhabitants".

There are of course many selectively-based pub guides covering the UK but each title in the Country Pubs & Inns series will provide the reader with the *most comprehensive* choice of pubs and inns in the countryside through handy-sized, county-based guides. The guide enables the reader to choose the pub or inn to visit based on his/her own criteria such as location, real ales served, food, entertainment etc.

This easy-to-use guide is divided into 7 chapters which allows the reader to select the area of Devon being visited. Each chapter begins with a map containing the numbered location of the pub or inn and a brief illustrated summary of the places of interest in the area. By using the number the reader can then find more information on their choice of pub or inn.

We do hope that you will enjoy visiting the pubs and inns contained in this guide. We are always interested in what our readers think of the pubs and inns covered (or not covered) in our guides so please do not hesitate to write to us using the reader reaction forms provided to the rear of the guide. Equally, you may contact us via our email address at info@travelpublishing.co.uk. This is a vital way of ensuring that we continue to provide a comprehensive list of pubs and inns to our readers.

Finally, if you are seeking visitor information on Devon or any other part of the British Isles we would like to refer you to the full list of Travel Publishing guides to be found at the rear of the book. You may also find more information about any of our titles on our website at www.travelpublishing.co.uk

Travel Publishing

How to use the guide

The *Country Pubs & Inns of Devon* provides details of pubs and inns (including hotels which welcome non-residents) situated in the countryside of Devon. "Countryside" is defined by *The Office of National Statistics* as "settlements of less than 10,000 inhabitants" so the much of Devon fulfills this definition!

This guide has been specifically designed as an easy-to-use guide so there is no need for complicated instructions. However the reader may find the following guidelines helpful in identifying the name, address, telephone number and facilities of the pub or inn.

Finding Pubs or Inns in a Selected Location

The guide is divided into 7 chapters (or sections) each covering a specific geographical area of Devon. Identify the area and page number you require from the map and table of contents on the following pages and turn to the relevant chosen page.

At the beginning of each chapter there is a detailed map of the area selected. The villages and towns denoted by **red** circles are places of interest on which information is provided in the introduction to the chapter should you wish to explore the area further. The numbered boxes in **green** represent each pub or inn in the area selected. For more information on the pub or inn simply locate the same number within the chapter (to the left of the pub/inn name) to find the name, address, telephone number and facilities of the pub or inn.

Finding a Specific Pub or Inn

If you know the name of the pub or inn and its location then simply go to the relevant chapter where the names of the pubs are listed in alphabetical order.

Pub and Inn Information

All pubs or inns in the guide give details of the name, address, telephone number and whether they offer real ales, food, accommodation and no smoking areas.

The advertising panels found in each chapter provide more comprehensive information on the pub or inn such as contact details, location, interior and exterior facilities, real ales, opening times, food, entertainment, disabled access, credit cards and places of interest.

Location Map

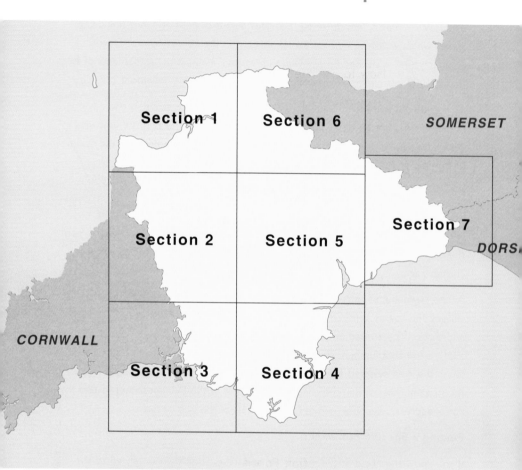

Contents

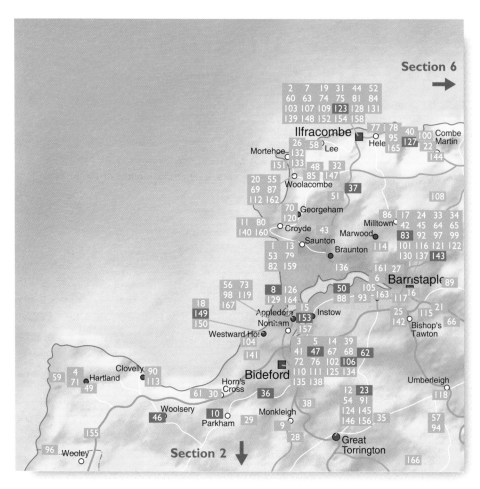

Section 6

2 7 19 31 44 52
60 63 74 75 81 84
103 107 109 123 128 131
139 148 152 154 158

Ilfracombe

77 78
95 165
40 100 Combe
127 22 Martin
144

Mortehoe
26 58 Lee
132
151 133 48 32
85 147
Hele

20 55
69 87
112 162
Woolacombe
37
51

70 120
Georgeham
11 80
140 160
Croyde 43
Saunton
Marwood
Braunton
1 13
53 79
82 159
136

86 17 24 33 34
42 45 64 65
83 92 97 99
101 116 121 122
130 137 143
Milltown

161 27
6
Barnstaple 89

56 73
98 119
167
8 126
129 164
50 105
88 93 163 117
6
25 115 21
142 66
Bishop's
Tawton

18 149 150
Appledore
Northam
15 153 157
Instow

Westward Ho!
104
141

3 5 14 39
41 47 67 68 62
72 76 102 106
110 111 125 134
135 138

Clovelly 90
59 4 71 49 Hartland 113
Horn's
Cross
61 30
36
38
12 23
54 91
124 145
146 156 35
Umberleigh
118

Woolsery
46
10
Parkham
29
Monkleigh
9
28
57 94

155

96 Wooley

Section 2

Great
Torrington

166

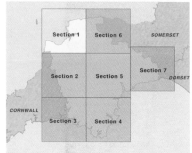

■	Pub or Inn Reference Number - Detailed Information
12	Pub or Inn Reference Number - Summary Entry
● ■	Place of interest mentioned in the chapter introduction

Section 1 Section 6 SOMERSET
Section 2 Section 5 Section 7
CORNWALL DORSET
Section 3 Section 4

2

NORTH DEVON COAST (WEST)

The wonderful stretch of North Devon's coastline between Hartland Point and Ilfracombe, the largest resort on the North Devon coast, takes in the irresistibly quaint village of Clovelly and the towns of Bideford and Barnstaple, lying at the mouths of the Rivers Torridge and Taw.

Appledore

Overlooking the Tor and Torridge estuaries, Appledore has been a thriving port since the 14th century. With such a history it is appropriate that it is the home of the **North Devon Maritime Museum**, housed in a former shipowner's home.

Barnstaple

Britain's oldest borough has plenty to attract the visitor, including the **Church of** **St Peter and St Paul**, the 17th century **Horwood's Almshouses**, the splendid **Heritage Centre** and the **Royal Barum Pottery**. Barnstaple is the northern terminus of the **Tarka Line** and the crossing point of the figure-of-eight **Tarka Trail**.

Bideford

Once Britain's third busiest port, specialising in the import of tobacco from North America. Evidence of this golden age can be seen in the many opulent merchant's houses that have survived. Charles Kingsley wrote his swashbuckling story *Westward Ho!* while staying at the Royal Hotel. Day trips can be arranged from Bideford to Lundy Island.

Braunton

Braunton Museum concentrates its displays and exhibits on village life and marine and agricultural history. Southwest of the village, **Braunton Great**

Long Bridge, Barnstaple

Field is a famous archaeological site, one of the few that displays the medieval system of strip farming. **Braunton Burrows** is a Site of Special Scientific Interest, the UK's premier dune system and home to nearly 500 varieties of plants.

Clovelly

This quaint and picturesque village, which tumbles down a steep hillside in terraced levels, is many people's idea of the typical Devonshire coastal village. Charles Kingsley was at school here in the 1820s and the **Kingsley Museum** illustrates the author's links with the village. **Fisherman's Cottage** provides a glimpse of what life was like here 80 years ago, and an audio-visual show in the **Visitor Centre** offers an informative introduction to Clovelly. Nearby is the **Milky Way Adventure Park** with entertainment for all the family;

it is also home to the **North Devon Bird of Prey Centre**.

Georgeham

Henry Williamson settled in a hilltop hut here after returning from World War I. It was here that he wrote his much-loved novel *Tarka the Otter*. Tarka lived in the land between the Taw and Torridge rivers, and many local places are featured in the story.

Great Torrington

The home of **Dartington Crystal**, where visitors can stroll through the factory shops and see the exhibition on the story of glass from the ancient Egyptians to the present day. During the Civil war the 'Cavalier Town' was the site of two small-scale clashes as well as the last major battle of the War, when over 17,000 troops fought in the streets. The story of the battle and the War is told at the **Torrington 1646 Exhibition** at Castle Hill. A mile south of Great Torrington is the Royal Horticultural Society Garden **Rosemoor** in a glorious setting in the Torridge Valley.

Hartland

Many fine Georgian houses survive in this pleasant village, but the most striking building hereabouts is the **Church of St Nectan**, a mile or so west of the village, reached down a path from the hamlet of Stoke. The glorious 15th

Cobbled Street, Clovelly

Ilfracombe

Instow

Railway buffs head for the **Instow Signal Box**, built in 1873 and restored as the first Grade II listed signal box in the country. South of Instow lie the 35-acre **Tapeley Park Gardens** on the eastern bank of the River Torridge.

Marwood

This ancient village is home to **Marwood Hill Gardens**, where 18 acres of pastureland have been transformed into a spectacular water garden with three lakes.

century screen, a masterpiece of the woodcarver's art, make this one of the most visited churches in the county. **Hartland Abbey** is home to a wonderful collection of paintings, porcelain and furniture, and the gardens are no less impressive. A helicopter service operates between Hartland Point and Lundy Island.

Ilfracombe

The largest resort on the north Devon coast, with attractions traditional and contemporary: **Holy Trinity Church**, the medieval **Chapel of St Nicholas**, the **Tunnel Beaches and Baths**, the fascinating **Aquarium** and the **Landmark Theatre and Arts Complex**.

Westward Ho!

The only place in the country named after a novel. Following the huge success of Charles Kingsley's tale, a company was formed in 1855 to develop this spectacular site with sandy beaches and rocky cliffs. The town is home to the unusual **Pot Walloping Festival**, when every spring locals and visitors throw pebbles dislodged during the winter storms back on to the famous ridge. Close by, the **Big Sheep** entertainment park is one of the Southwest's favourite family attractions.

1 The Agricultural Inn

East St, Braunton, Devon EX33 2EA
Tel: 01271 818001

Real Ales, Bar Food, Restaurant Menu,
No Smoking Area, Disabled Facilities

2 Altro Hotel

Fore St, Ilfracombe, Devon EX34 9DN
Tel: 01271 862096

Bar Food, Restaurant Menu, Accommodation,
No Smoking Area, Disabled Facilities

3 The Anchor

11 Honestone St, Bideford, Devon EX39 2DJ
Tel: 01237 425672

Bar Food

4 The Anchor Inn

Fore St, Hartland, Bideford, Devon EX39 6BD
Tel: 01237 441414

Real Ales, Bar Food, Restaurant Menu,
Accommodation, No Smoking Area

5 Appledore Inn

18 Chingswell St, Bideford, Devon EX39 2NF
Tel: 01237 472496

Real Ales, Bar Food

6 Barnstaple Hotel

Braunton Rd, Barnstaple, Devon EX31 1LE
Tel: 01271 376221

Bar Food, Restaurant Menu, Accommodation,
No Smoking Area, Disabled Facilities

7 Bath House Hotel

Runnacleave Rd, Ilfracombe, Devon EX34 8AR
Tel: 01271 866859

Bar Food, Restaurant Menu, Accommodation,
No Smoking Area

8 Beaver Inn

Irsha St, Appledore, Bideford, Devon EX39 1RY
Tel: 01237 474822

Real Ales, Bar Food, Restaurant Menu,
No Smoking Area, Disabled Facilities

See adjacent panel

8 The Beaver Inn

Irsha Street, Appledore, nr Bideford,
North Devon EX39 1RY
☎ 01237 474822

**Real Ales, Bar Food, Restaurant Menu,
No Smoking Area, Disabled Facilities**

- On the seafront at Appledore on the A386 3 miles N of Bideford
- 3 changing guests
- 12-2 & 6.30-9
- Live music Saturday
- Patio overlooking bay
- All the major cards
- 10-11 (Sun 12-10.30)
- Bideford 3 miles

Charming hosts Graham and Alison, smiling staff, home-cooked food and panoramic estuary views make the **Beaver Inn** one of the most delightful pubs in the region. The kitchen brigade, with Bob at the helm, prepare a selection of snacks and dishes highlighted by superb seafood specials. Malcolm assists, and few can resist Marjorie's scrumptious sweets.

9 The Bell Inn

Monkleigh, Bideford, Devon EX39 5JS
Tel: 01805 622338

Real Ales, Bar Food, Accommodation,
No Smoking Area, Disabled Facilities

10 The Bell Inn

Parkham, Bideford, Devon EX39 5PL
Tel: 01237 451201

Real Ales, Bar Food, Restaurant Menu,
Accommodation, No Smoking Area,
Disabled Facilities

See panel opposite

11 Billy Budds

12 Hobbs Hill, Croyde, Braunton,
Devon EX33 1LZ
Tel: 01271 890606

Bar Food, Restaurant Menu, Accommodation,
No Smoking Area

10 The Bell Inn

Rectory Lane, Parkham, nr Bideford,
Devon EX39 5PL

☎ 01237 451201

🌐 www.thebellinnparkham.co.uk

**Real Ales, Bar Food, Restaurant Menu,
Accommodation, No Smoking Area,
Disabled Facilities**

☞ From Bideford take the A39 towards Clovelly.
Left at Horns Cross towards Parkham,
through village and the inn is on the left

🍺 Bass, London Pride

🍴 12-1.30 & 6.30-9

🎵 Beer Festival first Sunday in June

🅿 Car park

💳 All the major cards

🕐 12-2 (Sun to 3) & 5.30-11 (Sun 6-10.30)

🏛 Horns Cross 1½ miles, Clovelly 7 miles,
Bideford 7 miles

The **Bell** is a 13th century thatched
building with cob walls, oak beams and
open fires. Local real ales and ciders are very
popular, and hosts Michael and Rachel have
the services of an excellent chef in Pauline,
whose repertoire runs from soups and pâtés
to locally landed fish specials, prime steaks
from Devon beef, seasonal game and
scrumptious sweets.

12 Black Horse

High St, Torrington, Devon EX38 8HN
Tel: 01805 622121

Real Ales, Bar Food, Restaurant Menu,
Accommodation, No Smoking Area,
Disabled Facilities

13 The Black Horse Inn

Church St, Braunton, Devon EX33 2EL
Tel: 01271 812386

Real Ales, Bar Food, No Smoking Area,
Disabled Facilities

14 Blacksmith Arms

23 Torrington St, Bideford, Devon EX39 4DP
Tel: 01237 477747

Real Ales, Bar Food, Disabled Facilities

15 Boathouse

Marine Parade, Bideford, Devon EX39 4JJ
Tel: 01271 861292

Real Ales, Bar Food, Restaurant Menu,
No Smoking Area, Disabled Facilities

16 The Borough Arms

Forches Avenue, Barnstaple, Devon EX32 8ED
Tel: 01271 328376

Bar Food, Restaurant Menu, Accommodation,
No Smoking Area, Disabled Facilities

17 Bridges Bar

3 Bridge Buildings, The Square, Barnstaple,
Devon EX32 8LW
Tel: 01271 321014

Bar Food

18 The Buccaneer

Bath Hotel Rd, Westward Ho, Bideford,
Devon EX39 1LE
Tel: 01237 424646

Real Ales

19 The Bunch Of Grapes

36 High St, Ilfracombe, Devon EX34 9DA
Tel: 01271 863276

Real Ales, Bar Food, No Smoking Area,
Disabled Facilities

20 Captain Jacks

Barton Rd, Woolacombe, Devon EX34 7BA
Tel: 01271 870648

Real Ales, No Smoking Area, Disabled Facilities

21 Castle Inn

Blakeshill Rd, Landkey, Barnstaple,
Devon EX32 0NF
Tel: 01271 830438

Real Ales, Bar Food, Restaurant Menu,
No Smoking Area, Disabled Facilities

22 The Castle Inn

High St, Combe Martin, Ilfracombe,
Devon EX34 0HS
Tel: 01271 883706

Real Ales, Bar Food, Restaurant Menu,
Accommodation, No Smoking Area,
Disabled Facilities

23 The Cavalier

Well Street, Great Torrington, Devon EX38 8EP
☎ 01805 623832

**Real Ales, Bar Food, Restaurant Menu,
Accommodation**

☛ At the bottom of the main street in Great
Torrington, 5 miles south of Bideford

🍺 Otter + guest

🍴 12-2 & 6-9

🛏 4 rooms (2 en suite)

🎵 Pool, darts

⚓ Beer garden, car park

💳 All the major cards

🕐 11-11

🏛 Dartington Glass, Weare Gifford Hall 1 mile,
RHS Rosemoor 1 mile, Bideford 5 miles

The **Cavalier** is a traditional pub at the foot
of the main street in Great Torringon. The
bar and garden are great places to enjoy a
drink, and a daily changing selection of dishes is
served in the restaurant. Overnight guests are
also catered for with four bedrooms.

23 The Cavalier Inn

Well St, Torrington, Devon EX38 8EP
Tel: 01805 623832

Real Ales, Bar Food, Restaurant Menu,
Accommodation

See panel adjacent

24 The Check Inn

14 Castle St, Barnstaple, Devon EX31 1DR
Tel: 01271 375964

Real Ales, Disabled Facilities

25 Chichester Arms

East St, Bishops Tawton, Barnstaple,
Devon EX32 0DQ
Tel: 01271 343945

Real Ales, Bar Food, Restaurant Menu,
No Smoking Area, Disabled Facilities

26 Chichester Arms

Mortehoe, Woolacombe, Devon EX34 7DU
Tel: 01271 870411

Real Ales, Bar Food, Restaurant Menu,
No Smoking Area, Disabled Facilities

27 The Chichester Arms

28 Pilton St, Barnstaple, Devon EX31 1PJ
Tel: 01271 375285

Real Ales, Bar Food, Restaurant Menu,
No Smoking Area, Disabled Facilities

28 Clinton Arms

Frithelstock, Torrington, Devon EX38 8JH
Tel: 01805 623279

Real Ales, Bar Food, Restaurant Menu,
Accommodation, No Smoking Area

29 Coach & Horses

Buckland Brewer, Bideford, Devon EX39 5LU
Tel: 01237 451395

Real Ales, Bar Food, Restaurant Menu,
No Smoking Area, Disabled Facilities

30 Coach & Horses Inn

Horns Cross, Bideford, Devon EX39 5DH
Tel: 01237 451214

Real Ales, Bar Food, Restaurant Menu,
Accommodation

31 Collingdale Hotel

13 Larkstone Terrace, Ilfracombe,
Devon EX34 9NU
Tel: 01271 863770

Bar Food, Restaurant Menu, Accommodation,
No Smoking Area

32 Cook Island

Mullacott Cross, Ilfracombe, Devon EX34 8NY
Tel: 01271 865500

Real Ales, Bar Food, Restaurant Menu,
No Smoking Area, Disabled Facilities

33 The Cork & Bottle

56 High St, Barnstaple, Devon EX31 1JB
Tel: 01271 323144

Real Ales, Bar Food, No Smoking Area

34 Corner House

108 Boutport St, Barnstaple, Devon EX31 1SY
Tel: 01271 343528

Real Ales, Disabled Facilities

35 Cranford Inn

St. Giles, Torrington, Devon EX38 7LA
Tel: 01805 623309

Real Ales, Bar Food, Restaurant Menu,
No Smoking Area

36 The Crealock Arms

Littleham, Bideford, Devon EX39 5HN
Tel: 01237 477065

Real Ales, Bar Food, Restaurant Menu,
No Smoking Area, Disabled Facilities

See panel below

---

36 The Crealock Arms

Littleham, nr Bideford, Devon EX39 5HN

☎ 01237 477065 ⊕ www.crealockarms.com

e-mail: clarick@brownmorg.fsnet.co.uk

**Real Ales, Bar Food, Restaurant Menu,
No Smoking Area, Disabled Facilities**

- ☛ 2 miles SW of Bideford off the A386
- 🍺 Crealock Ale
- 🍴 12-2.30 & 6.30-9.30; all day snacks
- 🎵 Darts
- ⛺ Garden, car park
- 💳 Major cards accepted
- 🕐 11.30-3.30 (Sun from 12) & 5.30-11.30 (Sun to 10.30)
- 🏛 Bideford 2 miles

Clare and Richard Morgan offer a warm welcome to customers old and new at the **Crealock Arms**, which was opened by Clare's grandparents in 1977. Crealock Ale, a light, hoppy brew, is a favourite tipple in the bar, where snacks can be enjoyed throughout the day. The main menu is served lunchtime and evening in the 64-cover restaurant, and the choice really does cater for all tastes, with sections for steaks, chicken, fish, vegetarian, pasta and chef's specials (delicious crispy pork noisettes with apple cider gravy). Light lunches and Beer Garden meals are available from 12 to 2.30. This fine old pub in a tiny village on the hills above the River Yeo was originally a farmhouse, and its name remembers General Crealock, a Victorian landowner and distinguished soldier. His grand monument stands in the village church.

37 The Crown Inn

West Down, Ilfracombe, Devon EX34 8NF
Tel: 01271 862790

Real Ales, Bar Food, Restaurant Menu,
No Smoking Area, Disabled Facilities

See panel below

38 Cyder Presse

Weare Giffard, Bideford, Devon EX39 4QR
Tel: 01237 425517

Real Ales, Bar Food, Restaurant Menu,
No Smoking Area, Disabled Facilities

37 The Crown

West Down, North Devon
☎ 01271 862790

**Real Ales, Bar Food, Restaurant Menu,
No Smoking Area, Disabled Facilities**

- ☛ West Down lies off the A361 between Ilfracombe and Braunton
- 🍺 Surf Board, Ring o' Bells Brewery
- 🍴 12-2 & 6-9
- 🏖 Large garden
- 💳 All the major cards
- 🕐 12-2 & 6-11
- 🏛 Ilfracombe 4 miles, Woolacombe 4 miles, Braunton 6 miles

The **Crown** is a fine old family-friendly pub with cheerful, relaxing ambience. Local real ales and a good choice of wines accompany landlord Ray Pearce's excellent  cooking, which includes daily specials and popular Sunday roasts. The Crown has ample off-road parking and a fantastic garden.

47 First In Last Out

27/28 Clovelly Road, Bideford,
Devon EX39 3BY
☎ 01237 474863

**Real Ales, Bar Food, Restaurant Menu,
No Smoking Area**

- ☛ 400 yards from the centre of Bideford on the road to Clovelly
- 🍺 Stand & Deliver
- 🍴 Food served daily
- 🎵 Quiz Sunday, games room, live bands
- 🏖 Beer garden
- 🕐 12-3 & 5.30-11 (all day Fri-Sun)
- 🏛 Westward Ho! 3 miles, Tapeley Park 4 miles

On the Clovelly Road on the outskirts of Bideford, **First In Last Out** is a popular pub with go-ahead hosts in Terry and Carol England.

In the cheerful bar the choice of real ales changes regularly, and an expanding selection of snacks and meals is available all day. The pub has a games room and beer garden.

39 Dj's Sports Bar

10 Cooper St, Bideford, Devon EX39 2DA
Tel: 01237 479858

Bar Food, No Smoking Area

40 The Dolphin Inn

Seaside, Combe Martin, Ilfracombe,
Devon EX34 0AW
Tel: 01271 883424

Real Ales, Bar Food, Restaurant Menu,
No Smoking Area, Disabled Facilities

41 East Of The Water

2 Barnstaple St, Bideford, Devon EX39 4AE
Tel: 01237 425329

Real Ales, Bar Food, Restaurant Menu,
No Smoking Area, Disabled Facilities

42 Ebberley Arms
Bear St, Barnstaple, Devon EX32 7BZ
Tel: 01271 342627

Bar Food, Restaurant Menu, Disabled Facilities

43 The Ebrington Arms
Knowle, Braunton, Devon EX33 2LW
Tel: 01271 812166

Real Ales, Bar Food, Restaurant Menu,
No Smoking Area, Disabled Facilities

44 Epchris Hotel
Torrs Park, Ilfracombe, Devon EX34 8AZ
Tel: 01271 862751

Restaurant Menu, Accommodation,
No Smoking Area, Disabled Facilities

45 Exeter Inn
12 Litchdon St, Barnstaple, Devon EX32 8ND
Tel: 01271 321709

Real Ales, Bar Food, Disabled Facilities

46 The Farmers Arms
Woolsery, Bideford, Devon EX39 5QS
Tel: 01237 431467

Real Ales, Bar Food, Restaurant Menu,
No Smoking Area

See panel below

47 First In Last Out
27-28 Clovelly Rd, Bideford, Devon EX39 3BY
Tel: 01237 474863

Real Ales, Bar Food, Restaurant Menu,
No Smoking Area

See panel opposite

48 Fortescue Arms
Station Rd, Woolacombe, Devon EX34 7HQ
Tel: 01271 870537

Real Ales, Bar Food, Restaurant Menu,
Accommodation, No Smoking Area,
Disabled Facilities

---

46 The Farmers Arms
Woolsery, nr Bideford, North Devon EX39 5QL
☎ 01237 431467

**Real Ales, Bar Food, Restaurant Menu,
No Smoking Area**

- Off the A39 8 miles W of Bideford
- Appledore and other local and national brews
- 12-9
- Quiz winter Tuesday
- Beer garden, car park
- Major cards accepted
- 12-11
- Clovelly 3 miles

Alan Lindsay, originally from Liverpool, was a regular customer at the **Farmers Arms** before buying the premises at the beginning of 2005. With his wife Jennie and their family, he runs this super little pub, where the oldest parts date back 800 years. Behind the immaculate thatched exterior, the bar and eating areas have an irresistible old-world charm, with ancient black beams on low ceilings and open fires to keep things cosy on even the coldest days. Brews from the local Appledore Brewery are among the several real ales always on tap, and sacks and full meals are served from noon to 9 o'clock in the evening. Jennie is a terrific cook, making excellent use of locally sourced produce in dishes like steak & ale or steak & mushroom pie, braised knuckle of lamb fish & chips and generous, healthy salads. Woolsery appears on some maps as Woolfardisworthy.

49 Fosfelle Country House Hotel

Hartland, Bideford, Devon EX39 6EF
Tel: 01237 441273

Bar Food, Restaurant Menu, Accommodation,
No Smoking Area, Disabled Facilities

50 **Fox & Hounds**

Fremington, Barnstaple, Devon EX31 2NT
Tel: 01271 373094

Real Ales, Bar Food, Disabled Facilities

See panel below

51 Foxhunters Inn

West Down, Ilfracombe, Devon EX34 8NU
Tel: 01271 863757

Real Ales, Bar Food, Restaurant Menu,
Accommodation, No Smoking Area,
Disabled Facilities

---

50 **The Fox & Hounds**

Church Hill, Fremington, nr Barnstaple,
Devon EX31 2NT

☎ 01271 373094

Real Ales, Bar Food, Disabled Facilities

☞ Off the B3233 3 miles west of Barnstaple, by
the Taw Estuary

🍺 Wadworths XXX

🍴 12-9

🎵 Traditional pub games, live music at the
weekend

⚓ Patio, car park

🕐 12-11

🏛 Taw Estuary; Tapeley Park 3 miles, Barnstaple 3
miles

Pat and Jane Oakey welcome one and all to
the family-friendly **Fox & Hounds**, an
honest, unpretentious pub close to the Taw
Estuary. The bar dispenses a wide selection of
drinks, and hot and cold snacks are served until
9 o'clock in the evening. Pool, darts, skittles and
shove-ha'penny are played at this sociable spot,
where a function room is available for parties.

---

52 George & Dragon

4 Fore St, Ilfracombe, Devon EX34 9ED
Tel: 01271 863851

Real Ales, Bar Food, Accommodation

53 The George Hotel

Exeter Rd, Braunton, Devon EX33 2JJ
Tel: 01271 812029

Real Ales, Accommodation, No Smoking Area,
Disabled Facilities

54 Globe Hotel

Fore St, Torrington, Devon EX38 8HQ
Tel: 01805 622220

Real Ales, Bar Food, Accommodation,
No Smoking Area

55 The Golden Hind

Beach Rd, Woolacombe, Devon EX34 7BP
Tel: 01271 871166

Real Ales, Bar Food, Restaurant Menu

56 The Golden Lion

38 Cross St, Northam, Bideford,
Devon EX39 1BS
Tel: 01237 474594

Real Ales

57 Golden Lion Inn

North Rd, High Bickington, Umberleigh,
Devon EX37 9BB
Tel: 01769 560213

Real Ales, Bar Food, Restaurant Menu,
Accommodation, No Smoking Area

58 The Grampus

Lee, Ilfracombe, Devon EX34 8LR
Tel: 01271 862906

Real Ales, Bar Food, Restaurant Menu,
No Smoking Area, Disabled Facilities

59 Hartland Quay Hotel

Stoke, Hartland, Bideford, Devon EX39 6DU
Tel: 01237 441218

Real Ales, Bar Food, Restaurant Menu,
Accommodation, No Smoking Area

60 The Hele Bay

39 Beach Rd, Ilfracombe, Devon EX34 9QZ
Tel: 01271 867795

Real Ales, Bar Food, Restaurant Menu,
Disabled Facilities

61 The Hoops Inn

Horns Cross, Bideford, Devon EX39 5DL
Tel: 01237 451222

Real Ales, Bar Food, Restaurant Menu,
Accommodation, No Smoking Area,
Disabled Facilities

62 Hunters Inn

Newton Tracey, Barnstaple, Devon EX31 3PL
Tel: 01271 858339

Real Ales, Bar Food, Restaurant Menu,
No Smoking Area, Disabled Facilities

Se panel adjacent

63 The Ilfracombe Carlton

Runnacleave Rd, Ilfracombe, Devon EX34 8AR
Tel: 01271 862446

Restaurant Menu, Accommodation,
No Smoking Area, Disabled Facilities

64 Imperial Hotel

Litchdon St, Barnstaple, Devon EX32 8NB
Tel: 01271 345861

Bar Food, Restaurant Menu, Accommodation,
No Smoking Area, Disabled Facilities

65 The Inn On The Square

The Square, Barnstaple, Devon EX32 8LS
Tel: 01271 311940

Bar Food, Restaurant Menu, Accommodation,
No Smoking Area, Disabled Facilities

66 The Jack Russell

Swimbridge, Barnstaple, Devon EX32 0PN
Tel: 01271 830366

Real Ales, Bar Food, Restaurant Menu,
Accommodation, No Smoking Area,
Disabled Facilities

67 Johnny's Bar

36 Mill St, Bideford, Devon EX39 2JJ
Tel: 01237 421105

Real Ales

68 Joiners Arms

Market Place, Bideford, Devon EX39 2DR
Tel: 01237 472675

Real Ales, Bar Food, Accommodation,
No Smoking Area, Disabled Facilities

69 The Jube

South St, Woolacombe, Devon EX34 7BB
Tel: 01271 870487

Bar Food, Disabled Facilities

62 The Hunters Inn

Newton Tracey, nr Bideford,
North Devon EX31 3PL
☎ 01271 858339

**Real Ales, Bar Food, Restaurant Menu,
No Smoking Area, Disabled Facilities**

☞ From Barnstaple (5 miles) A39 then B3232 to Newton Tracey.

🍺 Clearwater Village Pride

🍴 12-2 & 6.30-9

🎵 Quiz and Bingo Thursday

⛱ Garden, car park

💳 Major cards accepted

🕐 12-3 & 6-11

🏛 Tapeley Park 3 miles, Barnstaple 5 miles, Bideford 6 miles

On the B3232 a short drive south of Barnstaple, the **Hunters Inn** is a very pleasant village pub dating back to the 15th century. Hosts sally and Colin welcome visitors in the beamed bar, where the three real ales include Village Pride from the local Clearwater brewery. The inn is a popular spot for a snack or a meal (the steak & ale pie is a real winner) and when the sun shines the garden is the place to be.

70 Kings Arms
Georgeham, Braunton, Devon EX33 1JJ
Tel: 01271 890240

Real Ales, Bar Food, Disabled Facilities

71 The Kings Arms
Fore St Hartland, Bideford, Devon EX39 6BL
Tel: 01237 441222

Real Ales, Bar Food, Restaurant Menu,
No Smoking Area, Disabled Facilities

72 Kings Arms Hotel
The Quay, Bideford, Devon EX39 2HW
Tel: 01237 475196

Real Ales, Bar Food, Accommodation

73 Kingsley Inn
Fore St, Northam, Bideford, Devon EX39 1AW
Tel: 01237 474221

Real Ales, Disabled Facilities

74 La Bastille
Wilder Rd, Ilfracombe, Devon EX34 8BS
Tel: 01271 863726

Real Ales, Bar Food, Restaurant Menu,
No Smoking Area

75 The Lamb Hotel
59 High St, Ilfracombe, Devon EX34 9QB
Tel: 01271 863708

Real Ales, Bar Food, Accommodation

76 The Lamb Inn
83 Honestone St, Bideford, Devon EX39 2DH
Tel: 01237 472638

Disabled Facilities

77 Lee Bay Hotel
39 Beach Rd, Ilfracombe, Devon EX34 9QZ
Tel: 01271 867600

Real Ales, Bar Food, Restaurant Menu,
Accommodation, No Smoking Area,
Disabled Facilities

78 The Lodge Country House
Berrynarbor, Ilfracombe, Devon EX34 9SG
Tel: 01271 883246

Bar Food, Restaurant Menu, Accommodation,
No Smoking Area, Disabled Facilities

79 London Inn
17 Caen St, Braunton, Devon EX33 1AA
Tel: 01271 812603

Real Ales, Bar Food

80 Manor House Inn
39 St. Marys Rd, Croyde, Braunton,
Devon EX33 1PG
Tel: 01271 890241

Real Ales, Bar Food, Restaurant Menu,
Accommodation, No Smoking Area,
Disabled Facilities

81 Marine Court Hotel
Hillsborough Rd, Ilfracombe, Devon EX34 9QQ
Tel: 01271 862920

Accommodation, No Smoking Area

82 The Mariners Arms
42 South St, Braunton, Devon EX33 2AA
Tel: 01271 813160

Real Ales, Bar Food, Restaurant Menu,
No Smoking Area, Disabled Facilities

83 Marshals
95 Boutport St, Barnstaple, Devon EX31 1SX
Tel: 01271 376633

Real Ales, Bar Food, Disabled Facilities

See panel opposite

84 Merlin Court Hotel
Torrs Park, Ilfracombe, Devon EX34 8AY
Tel: 01271 862697

Bar Food, Restaurant Menu, Accommodation,
No Smoking Area, Disabled Facilities

83 Marshals

Boutport Street, Barnstaple, Devon EX31 1JX

☎ 01271 376633

Real Ales, Bar Food, Disabled Facilities

- ☞ Close to the centre of Barnstaple
- 🍺 Bass + guests
- 🍴 All day
- 🎵 Live music Sun from 3.30
- 💳 All the major cards
- 🕐 10am-11 (Sun from 12)
- 🏛 Close to all the attractions of Barnstaple

The Shingler family greet visitors to Marshals, their popular pub close to the centre of town. A mounted Hussar and his aide adorn the pub sign, and an array of flowers is an indication that this is a pub full of life and colour. Opening hours are from 10 o'clock till late Monday to Saturday and from noon on Sunday.

Live music starts at 3.30 on Sunday afternoons, but throughout the day and throughout the week the host of regular customers ensure that the place always buzzes. A selection of cask and other ales is always on tap at this Heavitree house, and coffee and sandwiches are available all day long, with more substantial daily dishes at lunchtime.

---

85 The Mill Inn

Woolacombe, Devon EX34 7HJ
Tel: 01271 870237

Real Ales, Bar Food, Restaurant Menu,
No Smoking Area, Disabled Facilities

86 Muddiford Inn

Muddiford, Barnstaple, Devon EX31 4EY
Tel: 01271 850243

Real Ales, Restaurant Menu, No Smoking Area,
Disabled Facilities

87 Narracott Hotel

Beach Rd, Woolacombe, Devon EX34 7BS
Tel: 01271 870418

Bar Food, Restaurant Menu, Accommodation,
No Smoking Area, Disabled Facilities

88 The New Inn

Fremington, Barnstaple, Devon EX31 2NT
Tel: 01271 373859

Real Ales, Bar Food, Restaurant Menu,
No Smoking Area

89 The New Inn

Goodleigh, Barnstaple, Devon EX32 7LX
Tel: 01271 342488

Real Ales, Bar Food, Restaurant Menu,
No Smoking Area

90 New Inn Hotel

High St, Clovelly, Bideford, Devon EX39 5TQ
Tel: 01237 431303

Real Ales, Bar Food, Restaurant Menu,
Accommodation, No Smoking Area,
Disabled Facilities

91 Newmarket Inn
10 South St, Torrington, Devon EX38 8HE
Tel: 01805 622289

Real Ales, Accommodation, No Smoking Area,
Disabled Facilities

92 North Country Inn
128 Boutport St, Mermaid Walk, Barnstaple,
Devon EX31 ITD
Tel: 01271 376192

Real Ales, Bar Food, Restaurant Menu,
No Smoking Area

93 The Old Barn Inn
Tews Lane, Bickington, Barnstaple,
Devon EX31 2JU
Tel: 01271 372195

Real Ales, Bar Food, Restaurant Menu,
No Smoking Area

94 Old George Inn
High Bickington, Umberleigh, Devon EX37 9AY
Tel: 01769 560513

Real Ales, Bar Food, Restaurant Menu,
No Smoking Area, Disabled Facilities

95 The Old Sawmill Inn
Berrynarbor, Ilfracombe, Devon EX34 9SX
Tel: 01271 882259

Real Ales, Bar Food, Restaurant Menu,
No Smoking Area, Disabled Facilities

96 The Old Smithy Inn
Welcombe, Bideford, Devon EX39 6HG
Tel: 01288 331305

Real Ales, Bar Food, Restaurant Menu,
No Smoking Area, Disabled Facilities

97 The Olive Branch
41 Boutport St, Barnstaple, Devon EX31 ISE
Tel: 01271 370784

Bar Food, Restaurant Menu, No Smoking Area

98 The Olive Tree
Heywood Rd, Northam, Bideford,
Devon EX39 3QB
Tel: 01237 472361

Bar Food, Restaurant Menu, Accommodation,
Disabled Facilities

99 P.V.'S
Boutport St, Barnstaple, Devon EX31 IHG
Tel: 01271 342449

Bar Food, Restaurant Menu

100 Pack O'cards Inn
High St, Combe Martin, Ilfracombe,
Devon EX34 0ET
Tel: 01271 882300

Real Ales, Bar Food, Restaurant Menu,
Accommodation, No Smoking Area

101 The Panniers
33 Boutport St, Barnstaple, Devon EX31 IRX
Tel: 01271 329720

Real Ales, Bar Food, Restaurant Menu,
No Smoking Area, Disabled Facilities

102 Patch & Parrot
5 Cooper St, Bideford, Devon EX39 2DA
Tel: 01237 473648

Real Ales

103 The Pier
The Pier, The Quay, Ilfracombe,
Devon EX34 9EQ
Tel: 01271 866225

Real Ales, Bar Food, Restaurant Menu,
No Smoking Area, Disabled Facilities

104 The Pig On The Hill
West Pusehill, Westward Ho, Bideford,
Devon EX39 5AH
Tel: 01237 425889

Real Ales, Bar Food, Restaurant Menu,
No Smoking Area, Disabled Facilities

105 The Plough Inn
Bickington, Barnstaple, Devon EX31 2JG
Tel: 01271 343176

Real Ales, Bar Food, Disabled Facilities

106 Portobello Inn
37 Silver St, Bideford, Devon EX39 2DY
Tel: 01237 421990

Real Ales, Bar Food, Restaurant Menu,
No Smoking Area, Disabled Facilities

See panel opposite

106 The Portobello Inn

37 Silver Street, Bideford, Devon EX39 2DY

☎ 01237 421990

**Real Ales, Bar Food, Restaurant Menu,
No Smoking Area, Disabled Facilities**

☛ Close to the Pannier Market in Bideford

🍺 Bass, rotating local brews

🍴 12-6 (Sun 12.30-3); snacks all day

🎵 Quiz Thursday

🚗 Major cards accepted

🕐 11-11

🏛 Attractions of Bideford, coast and country walks

The **Portobello Inn** is a substantial black-and-white building near the famous Pannier Market in the attractive town of Bideford.

Local brews are rotated on a regular basis in the bar, and traditional pub favourites are served throughout the day in a pleasant contemporary setting. Thursday is quiz night.

107 Prince Of Wales

2 Fore St, Ilfracombe, Devon EX34 9ED
Tel: 01271 866391

Real Ales, Bar Food, Disabled Facilities

108 The Pyne Arms

East Down, Barnstaple, Devon EX31 4LX
Tel: 01271 850207

Real Ales, Bar Food, Restaurant Menu,
No Smoking Area, Disabled Facilities

109 Queens Tardis Inn

106 High St, Ilfracombe, Devon EX34 9ET
Tel: 01271 865790

Real Ales

110 Quigleys

1 Bridgeland St, Bideford, Devon EX39 2PS
Tel: 01237 477466

Real Ales, Bar Food, Restaurant Menu,
No Smoking Area

111 Quigleys Custom House

1 Bridgeland St, Bideford, Devon EX39 2PS
Tel: 01237 425267

Real Ales, Bar Food, Restaurant Menu,
No Smoking Area, Disabled Facilities

112 The Red Barn

Barton Rd, Woolacombe, Devon EX34 7DF
Tel: 01271 870264

Real Ales, Bar Food, Restaurant Menu,
No Smoking Area

113 The Red Lion

The Quay, Clovelly, Bideford, Devon EX39 5TF
Tel: 01237 431237

Real Ales, Bar Food, Restaurant Menu,
Accommodation, No Smoking Area

114 The Ring O Bell

Prixford, Barnstaple, Devon EX31 4DX
Tel: 01271 343836

Real Ales, Bar Food, Restaurant Menu,
Accommodation, No Smoking Area,
Disabled Facilities

115 The Ring O Bells

Landkey, Barnstaple, Devon EX32 0JJ
Tel: 01271 830364

Real Ales, Bar Food, Restaurant Menu,
No Smoking Area, Disabled Facilities

116 The Rising Sun

87 Boutport St, Barnstaple, Devon EX31 1SR
Tel: 01271 327102

No Smoking Area

117 The Rising Sun

29 Newport Rd, Barnstaple, Devon EX32 9BQ
Tel: 01271 342666

Real Ales, Bar Food, No Smoking Area,
Disabled Facilities

118 The Rising Sun Inn

Umberleigh, Devon EX37 9DU
Tel: 01769 560447

Real Ales, Bar Food, Restaurant Menu,
Accommodation, No Smoking Area,
Disabled Facilities

119 Riversford Hotel

Limers Lane, Northam, Bideford,
Devon EX39 2RG
Tel: 01237 474239

Real Ales, Restaurant Menu, Accommodation,
No Smoking Area, Disabled Facilities

120 Rockinn

Rock Hill, Georgeham, Braunton,
Devon EX33 1JW
Tel: 01271 890322

Real Ales, Bar Food, No Smoking Area

121 The Rose & Crown

52 Newport Rd, Barnstaple, Devon EX32 9BQ
Tel: 01271 343802

Real Ales, Bar Food, Accommodation,
No Smoking Area

122 Royal & Fortescue Hotel & The Bank

Boutport St, Barnstaple, Devon EX31 1HG
Tel: 01271 324446

Restaurant Menu, Accommodation,
No Smoking Area

123 Royal Britannia Hotel & Restaurant

Broad St, Ilfracombe, Devon EX34 9EE
Tel: 01271 862939

Real Ales, Restaurant Menu, Accommodation,
No Smoking Area, Disabled Facilities

See panel below

124 The Royal Exchange

86 New St, Torrington, Devon EX38 8BT
Tel: 01805 623395

Real Ales, Bar Food, No Smoking Area,
Disabled Facilities

---

123 The Royal Britannia

Broad Street, Ilfracombe,
North Devon EX34 9EE

☎ 01271 862939

**Real Ales, Restaurant Menu, Accommodation,
No Smoking Area, Disabled Facilities**

- ☞ Right by the harbour in Ilfracombe
- 🍺 Bass
- 🍴 12-2 & 5-9
- 🛏 18 rooms
- ⛱ Terrace
- 💳 Major cards accepted
- 🕐 11-11 (Sun 12-10.30)
- 🏛 South West Coast Path; Exmoor 4 miles, surfing beaches at Woolacombe (5 miles) and Croyde (10 miles)

The largest seaside resort on the North Devon coast is a great place for a holiday, and the **Royal Britannia** makes an ideal base. Comfortably traditional yet thoroughly up to date, the hotel enjoys a superb setting overlooking the harbour, and resident proprietors Anne and Bob Gilbourne have a warm and genuine welcome for all their guests. The 18 bedrooms abundant comfort and fine views, and the hotel has two bars and a capacious terrace from where guests can watch the comings and going in the busy harbour. Coffees, teas and light snacks are served all day, and the main menu is available every lunchtime and evening. The choice covers meat, fish and vegetarian options, a children's menu and a good range of desserts. The hotel can make arrangements with experienced skippers for deep-sea fishing trips.

125 Royal George Inn

Meeting St, Bideford, Devon EX39 1RJ
Tel: 01237 474335

Real Ales, Bar Food, Restaurant Menu,
No Smoking Area, Disabled Facilities

126 The Royal Hotel

Bude St, Appledore, Bideford, Devon EX39 1PS
Tel: 01237 474305

Real Ales, Bar Food, Restaurant Menu,
No Smoking Area

127 The Royal Marine

Seaside, Combe Martin, Ilfracombe,
Devon EX34 0AW
Tel: 01271 882470

Real Ales, Bar Food, Restaurant Menu,
Accommodation, No Smoking Area,
Disabled Facilities

See panel below

128 The Sandpiper Inn

The Quay, Ilfracombe, Devon EX34 9EQ
Tel: 01271 865260

Real Ales, Bar Food, Restaurant Menu,
No Smoking Area

129 Seagate Hotel

The Quay, Appledore, Bideford,
Devon EX39 1QS
Tel: 01237 472589

Real Ales, Bar Food, Restaurant Menu,
Accommodation, No Smoking Area,
Disabled Facilities

130 Seamus Odonnells

29 Boutport St, Barnstaple, Devon EX31 1RP
Tel: 01271 322177

Real Ales

127 The Royal Marine

Seaside Avenue, Combe Martin,
North Devon EX34 0AW

☎ 01271 882470   🌐 www.theroyalmarine.co.uk

**Real Ales, Bar Food, Restaurant Menu,
Accommodation, No Smoking Area,
Disabled Facilities**

☛ On the seafront at Combe Martin (A399)

🍺 Changing selection

🍴 12-2 & 6-9

🛏 6 en suite rooms

🅿 Car park

💳 Major cards accepted

🕐 11-11 (Sun 12-10.30)

🏛 Beach short walk; Camborne Wildlife &
Dinosaur Park 1 mile, Parracombe 4 miles,
Lynton and Lynmouth 8 miles

Overlooking the Bay on the seafront at
Combe Martin, the **Royal Marine**
combines the very best features of a public
house, restaurant and seaside hotel. It's equally
popular with locals and the many visitors to
the region, and a warm welcome is guaranteed
for everyone from top hosts Patricia and
Mervyn Lethaby. The bar is well stocked with
real ales, keg beers, ciders, wines, spirits ands
soft drinks, and residents and non-residents can
enjoy a varied, appetising menu of home-
cooked dishes. Pat heads a bust team in the
kitchen, gaining an ever-widening reputation for
the quality of the cooking, which uses the very
best local produce wherever possible. The
Royal Marine has six well-appointed guest
bedrooms, with views of the beach, Hangmans
Cliff or both.

131 Ship & Pilot

10 Broad St, Ilfracombe, Devon EX34 9EE
Tel: 01271 863562

Real Ales

132 Ship Aground Inn

Mortehoe, Woolacombe, Devon EX34 7DT
Tel: 01271 870856

Real Ales, Bar Food

133 Smugglers Rest

North Morte Rd, Mortehoe, Woolacombe,
Devon EX34 7DR
Tel: 01271 870891

Real Ales, Bar Food, Restaurant Menu,
Accommodation, No Smoking Area

134 Swan Inn

49 Torrington St, Bideford, Devon EX39 4DP
Tel: 01237 473460

Real Ales, Bar Food, Restaurant Menu,
Accommodation

135 Tantons Hotel

New Rd, Bideford, Devon EX39 2HR
Tel: 01237 473317

Real Ales, Bar Food, Restaurant Menu,
Accommodation, No Smoking Area,
Disabled Facilities

136 Tarka Inn

Braunton Rd, Heanton, Barnstaple,
Devon EX31 4AX
Tel: 01271 816547

Real Ales, Bar Food, Restaurant Menu,
No Smoking Area

137 The Tavern

1 Diamond St, Barnstaple, Devon EX32 8NA
Tel: 01271 324704

Real Ales, Bar Food, Restaurant Menu,
Disabled Facilities

138 The Tavern In The Port

1-3 Bridge St, Bideford, Devon EX39 2BU
Tel: 01237 423334

Bar Food

139 The Terrace Tapas & Wine Bar

62 Fore St, Ilfracombe, Devon EX34 9ED
Tel: 01271 863482

Real Ales, Bar Food, Restaurant Menu,
No Smoking Area, Disabled Facilities

140 The Thatched Barn Inn

14 Hobbs Hill, Croyde, Braunton,
Devon EX33 1LZ
Tel: 01271 890349

Real Ales, Bar Food, Restaurant Menu,
Accommodation, Disabled Facilities

143 The Three Tuns Inn

80 High Street, Barnstaple, Devon EX31 1HX
☎ 01271 371308

**Real Ales, Bar Food, Restaurant Menu,
No Smoking Area, Disabled Facilities**

☞ On the main street of town

🍺 2 rotating guests

🍴 10-9.30

🎵 Elizabethan theme entertainment

🕐 10am-11

🏛 Close to all the attractions of Barnstaple

On the main street of historic Barnstaple, the **Three Tuns Inn** brings history up to date. Behind the period frontage with small-paned windows and galleried upper floor, the inn has been refurbished with an Elizabethan theme: décor, staff costumes, cooking the lot!

141 The Thatched Inn

Abbotsham, Bideford, Devon EX39 5BA
Tel: 01237 471321

Real Ales, Bar Food, Restaurant Menu,
No Smoking Area, Disabled Facilities

142 Three Pigeons

Village St, Bishops Tawton, Barnstaple,
Devon EX32 0DG
Tel: 01271 372269

Real Ales, Bar Food, Restaurant Menu,
Accommodation, No Smoking Area,
Disabled Facilities

143 Three Tuns

80 High St, Barnstaple, Devon EX31 1HX
Tel: 01271 371308

Real Ales, Bar Food, Restaurant Menu,
No Smoking Area, Disabled Facilities

See panel below

144 The Top George Inn

Victoria St, Combe Martin, Ilfracombe,
Devon EX34 0LZ
Tel: 01271 883564

Bar Food, No Smoking Area

145 Torridge Inn

Mill St, Torrington, Devon EX38 8AW
Tel: 01805 625267

Real Ales, Bar Food, Restaurant Menu,
No Smoking Area

146 Torrington Arms

New St, Torrington, Devon EX38 8BX
Tel: 01805 622280

Real Ales, Bar Food, Accommodation,
Disabled Facilities

149 The Village Inn

Youngaton Road, Westward Ho!,
North Devon EX39 1HU

☎ 01237 477331   ⊕ www.hudsonsvillageinn.co.uk

**Real Ales, Bar Food, Restaurant Menu,
Accommodation, No Smoking Area,
Disabled Facilities**

☛ From the A39 turn right off A39/A386, then
B3236 to Westward Ho!

🍺 Otter, Butcombe

🍴 12-2 & 7-9 (6.30-9.30 summer)

🛏 4 en suite rooms

🎵 Pétanque, pool, darts

⚓ Patio, car park

💳 Major cards accepted

🕐 11-11 (Sun 12-10.30)

🏛 North Devon & Somerset Coastal Path;
Bideford 2 miles, Tapeley Park 4 miles

Visitors to this delightful inn near the
seafront at Westward Ho! will confirm the
resident hosts' proud boast that this really is
'everything a **Village Inn** should be'. Julie and
Stuart Hudson and their daughter make guests
feel instantly at home in this friendly place,
where the four en suite guest bedrooms are
warm, comfortable and very well equipped. A
hearty English breakfast is served in the intimate
restaurant, where lunches and dinners highlight
fresh Devon produce on wide-ranging menus.
The restaurant and conservatory are non-
smoking areas, as are the bedrooms. The inn is
also a splendid place to pause for a drink (real
ales on tap) and a snack, either in the bar or
outside in the patio garden.

147 Trimstone Manor Hotel

Trimstone, West Down, Ilfracombe,
Devon EX34 8NR
Tel: 01271 862841

Restaurant Menu, Accommodation,
No Smoking Area

148 Victoria Hotel

145 High St, Ilfracombe, Devon EX34 9EZ
Tel: 01271 863753

Real Ales, No Smoking Area

149 The Village Inn

Youngaton Rd, Westward Ho, Bideford,
Devon EX39 1HU
Tel: 01237 477331

Real Ales, Bar Food, Restaurant Menu,
Accommodation, No Smoking Area,
Disabled Facilities

See panel on page 21

150 The Waterfront Inn

Golf Links Rd, Westward Ho, Bideford,
Devon EX39 1LH
Tel: 01237 474737

Real Ales, Accommodation, Disabled Facilities

151 Watersmeet Hotel Ltd

Mortehoe, Woolacombe, Devon EX34 7EB
Tel: 01271 870333

Bar Food, Restaurant Menu, Accommodation, ,
No Smoking Area, Disabled Facilities

152 The Waverley

19 St. James Place, Ilfracombe, Devon EX34 9BJ
Tel: 01271 862681

Real Ales, Bar Food, Disabled Facilities

153 The Wayfarer Inn

Lane End, Instow, Bideford, Devon EX39 4LB
Tel: 01271 860342

Real Ales, Bar Food, Restaurant Menu,
No Smoking Area, Disabled Facilities

See panel adjacent

153 The Wayfarer Inn

Lane End, Instow Seafront, nr Bideford,
Devon EX39 4LB
☎ 01271 860342

**Real Ales, Bar Food, Restaurant Menu,
No Smoking Area, Disabled Facilities**

☛ Just back from the seafront on the B3253 3 miles NE of Bideford

🍺 Doom Bar, Tawny

🍴 12-3 & 6-9; all day snacks

🛏 9 en suite rooms

🎵 Live music Fri, quiz Sun in winter

🌳 Beer garden

💳 All the major cards

🕐 11-11 (Sun 12-10.30)

🏛 Instow Signal Box 1 mile, Tapeley Park 1 mile, Bideford 3 miles

A warm welcome, real ales, great food and a suntrap beer garden makes the Wayfarer Inn very popular. Proprietor Royston Dennis owns fishing boats, so the seafood specials really couldn't be fresher. Just yards from the beach at Instow, the family-friendly Wayfarer also has 9 en suite bedrooms.

154 The Wellington

66-67 High St, Ilfracombe, Devon EX34 9QE
Tel: 01271 862206

Real Ales

155 West Country Inn

Hartland, Bideford, Devon EX39 6HB
Tel: 01237 441724

Real Ales, Bar Food, Restaurant Menu,
Accommodation, No Smoking Area,
Disabled Facilities

156 The West Of England Inn

18 South St, Torrington, Devon EX38 8AA
Tel: 01805 624949

Real Ales, Bar Food, Restaurant Menu,
Accommodation, No Smoking Area

157 Westleigh Inn

Westleigh, Bideford, Devon EX39 4NL
Tel: 01271 860867

Real Ales, Bar Food, Restaurant Menu,
No Smoking Area, Disabled Facilities

158 Wheel Room Inn & Restaurant

The Promanade, Ilfracombe, Devon EX34 8AU
Tel: 01271 862545

Real Ales, Bar Food, Restaurant Menu,
Accommodation, No Smoking Area

159 White Lion Inn

North St, Braunton, Devon EX33 1AJ
Tel: 01271 813085

Real Ales, Restaurant Menu

160 The Whiteleaf At Croyde

Croyde, Braunton, Devon EX33 1PN
Tel: 01271 890266

Restaurant Menu, Accommodation,
No Smoking Area

161 The Windsor Arms

55 Bradiford, Bradiford, Barnstaple,
Devon EX31 4AD
Tel: 01271 343583

Real Ales, Bar Food, Restaurant Menu,
No Smoking Area, Disabled Facilities

162 The Woolacombe Bay Hotel

Woolacombe Bay Hotel, Woolacombe,
Devon EX34 7BN
Tel: 01271 870388

Bar Food, Accommodation, No Smoking Area,
Disabled Facilities

163 The Wrey Arms

Bickington Rd, Sticklepath, Barnstaple,
Devon EX31 2BX
Tel: 01271 376000

Real Ales, Bar Food, Restaurant Menu,
Accommodation, No Smoking Area

164 Ye Champion Of Wales

Meeting St, Appledore, Bideford,
Devon EX39 1RJ
Tel: 01237 425993

Real Ales, Disabled Facilities

165 Ye Olde Globe Inn

Berrynarbor, Ilfracombe, Devon EX34 9SG
Tel: 01271 882465

Real Ales, Bar Food, No Smoking Area

166 Ye Olde Inne

Roborough, Winkleigh, Devon EX19 8SY
Tel: 01805 603247

Real Ales, Bar Food, Restaurant Menu,
No Smoking Area

167 Yeoldon House Hotel

Durrant Lane, Northam, Bideford,
Devon EX39 2RL
Tel: 01237 474400

Restaurant Menu, Accommodation,
No Smoking Area

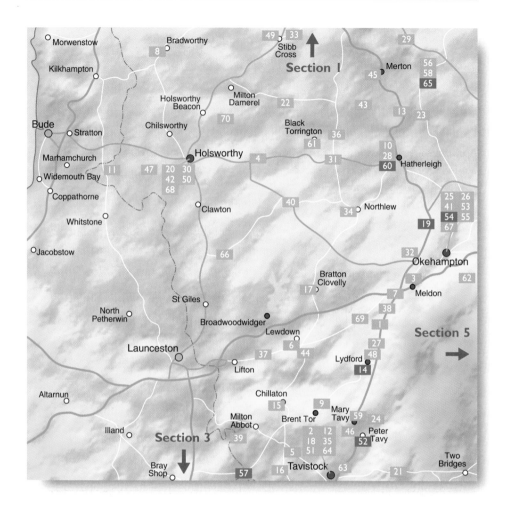

Morwenstow
Bradworthy
49 33
Stibb
Cross
8
29
Section 1
Kilkhampton
Merton 56
45 58
65
Holsworthy
Beacon
Milton
Damerel
22
43
13 23
Chilsworthy
70
Black
Torrington
36
Bude
Stratton
Holsworthy
61
10
28
Marhamchurch
4
31
60 Hatherleigh
Widemouth Bay
11 47 20 30
42 50
68
25 26
41 53
54 55
67
Coppathorne
Clawton
40
Northlew
34
19
Whitstone
Jacobstow
66
32
Okehampton
Bratton
Clovelly
St Giles
17
62
North
Petherwin
Broadwoodwidger
3
7 Meldon
Lewdown
38
69
Launceston
6
1 Section 5
37 44
27
Lifton
48
Lydford
14
Chillaton
Altarnun
15
9 Mary
Tavy 59
Milton
Abbot
Brent Tor
24
Illand
Section 3
39
2 12 46 Peter
18 35 52 Tavy
5 51 64
Bray
Shop
57 16 Tavistock 63 21
Two
Bridges

11 Pub or Inn Reference Number - Detailed Information

12 Pub or Inn Reference Number - Summary Entry

● ■ Place of interest mentioned in the chapter introduction

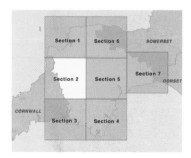

CENTRAL DEVON NORTH

A picturesque and less visited part of the county, with Holsworthy, close to the Cornish border, Okehampton, which once had the largest cathedral in Devon, and Tavistock at its southern extremity the main towns.

Brent Tor

Brent Tor, a volcanic plug rising 1,100 feet, is one of the most striking sights in the whole of Dartmoor. On its summit stands the medieval **Church of St Michael de Rupe**. This is the fourth smallest complete church in England – it measures just 15 feet in width and 37 feet in length, and although its walls are just 10 feet high they are three feet thick. The summit is sometimes lost in cloud, but when the skies are clear visitors are rewarded with magnificent views of Dartmoor, Bodmin Moor and the sea at Plymouth Sound. The West Devon Way and the Coast-to-Coast Cycle Way both pass through the village of North Brentor.

Broadwoodwidger

Roadford Lake, a reservoir completed in 1990, has a network of footpaths and a section designated a Special Protection Zone to allow wildlife a safe haven. Close to the village, **Dingles Steam Village** offers an insight into the area's industrial heritage in 20,000 square feet of indoor displays.

Hatherleigh

The 15th century **Church of St John the Baptist** survived the fire of 1840 that destroyed much of Hatherleigh's ancient centre, but in 1990 its spindly wooden spire collapsed in a gale. Now fully restored, the church, set high above the Lew Valley, continues to provide a striking focal point of this pleasant rural community. **Hatherleigh Pottery and Stock in Trade Textiles** is a working studio and art gallery.

Dartmoor Ponies

Holsworthy

A well-established agricultural centre with a weekly traditional street market and the annual St Peter's Fair. It lies on the 250-mile West Country Way cycle path.

Lydford

In Saxon times, Lydford was one of just 4 royal boroughs in Devon, along with Exeter, Barnstaple and Totnes. What made it so important was its

White Lady Waterfall, Lydford

strategic position on the River Lyd, and the Normans built a fortification that was superseded by the present **Lydford Castle**. Southwest of the village, the valley of the Lyd suddenly narrows to form the mile-and-a-half **Lydford Gorge**, one of Dartmoor's most spectacular natural features.

Mary Tavy

Named after its church and the nearby river, this old industrial village is situated in the heart of Dartmoor's former lead, tin and copper mining country. A mile to the north stands one of the most evocative reminders of those days – Wheal Betsy, a restored pumping engine house dating from the 18th century.

Meldon

On the Dartmoor Railway, **Meldon Viaduct Station** is the highest in southern England. A Visitor Centre tells the story of the railway, the viaduct and Meldon Quarry.

Merton

A remarkable museum here – the **Barometer World and Museum**, with

the largest public display of English barometers in the world. This remarkable collection was begun by Edwin Banfield, a retired bank manager, in the early 1970s.

Okehampton

Once the largest in Devon, **Okehampton Castle** remains imposing even in ruins, and the massive keep stands tall in its hilltop setting. Other interesting buildings include the 15th century **Chapel of Ease**, the **Town Hall**, the **Museum of Exmoor Life** and the beautifully restored **Railway Station**. To the south stand the great Dartmoor peaks of **High Willhays** and **Yes Tor**.

Tavistock

A handsome market town that became one of the four stannary towns (Ashburton, Chagford, Plympton) after tin was discovered in the 13th century. Little of the town's 10th century abbey remains, but the medieval parish church still stands. A market takes place every Friday in the splendid **Pannier Market**, while the **Goose Fair**, a wonderful, traditional street fair, is held every year in October.

1 Bearslake Inn

Lake, Sourton, Okehampton, Devon EX20 4HQ
Tel: 01837 861334

Real Ales, Bar Food, Restaurant Menu,
Accommodation, No Smoking Area,
Disabled Facilities

2 Bedford Hotel

1 Plymouth Rd, Tavistock, Devon PL19 8BB
Tel: 01822 613221

Real Ales, Bar Food, Restaurant Menu,
Accommodation, No Smoking Area

3 Betty Cottles Inn

Tavistock Rd, Okehampton, Devon EX20 4LR
Tel: 01837 55339

Real Ales, Bar Food, Restaurant Menu,
Accommodation, No Smoking Area,
Disabled Facilities

4 Bickford Arms

Bickford Arms, Brandis Corner, Holsworthy,
Devon EX22 7XY
Tel: 01409 221318

Real Ales, Bar Food, Restaurant Menu,
Accommodation, No Smoking Area,
Disabled Facilities

5 The Blacksmiths Arms

Lamerton, Tavistock, Devon PL19 8QR
Tel: 01822 612962

Real Ales, Bar Food, Restaurant Menu,
No Smoking Area, Disabled Facilities

6 Blue Lion Hotel

Lewdown, Okehampton, Devon EX20 4DL
Tel: 01566 783238

Real Ales, Bar Food

7 Bottleneck Inn

Church Rd, Sourton Down, Okehampton,
Devon EX20 4HT
Tel: 01837 861349

Real Ales, Bar Food, Restaurant Menu,
Accommodation, No Smoking Area,
Disabled Facilities

8 Bradworthy Inn

The Square, Bradworthy, Holsworthy,
Devon EX22 7TD
Tel: 01409 241222

Real Ales, Bar Food, Restaurant Menu,
Accommodation, No Smoking Area,
Disabled Facilities

9 The Brentor Inn

Brentor, Tavistock, Devon PL19 0NF
Tel: 01822 811001

Real Ales, Bar Food, Restaurant Menu,
Accommodation, No Smoking Area

10 Bridge Inn

Bridge St, Hatherleigh, Okehampton,
Devon EX20 3JA
Tel: 01837 810947

Real Ales, Bar Food, Restaurant Menu,
Accommodation, No Smoking Area,
Disabled Facilities

11 The Bridge Inn

Bridgerule, Holsworthy, Devon EX22 7EJ
Tel: 01288 381316

Real Ales

12 Browns Hotel

80 West St, Tavistock, Devon PL19 8AQ
Tel: 01822 618686

Real Ales, Bar Food, Restaurant Menu,
Accommodation, No Smoking Area,
Disabled Facilities

13 The Bull & Dragon

Meeth, Okehampton, Devon EX20 3EP
Tel: 01837 810325

Real Ales, Restaurant Menu, Accommodation,
No Smoking Area, Disabled Facilities

14 The Castle Inn & Hotel

Lydford, Okehampton, Devon EX20 4BH
Tel: 01822 820242

Real Ales, Bar Food, Restaurant Menu,
Accommodation, No Smoking Area

See panel on page 28

14 The Castle Inn

Lydford, nr Okehampton, Devon EX20 4BH

☎ 01822 820241/2   🌐 www.castleinnlydford.co.uk

**Real Ales, Bar Food, Restaurant Menu,
Accommodation, No Smoking Area**

- ☛ Off the A386 Okehampton to Tavistock road
- 🍺 Selection
- 🍴 12-2, 6.30-9 Daily
- 🛏 8 en-suite rooms
- 🎵 Quiz night every Wednesday
- ⛏ Parking
- 💳 Mastercard, Visa
- 🚫 No smoking in dining area
- 🕐 11-11
- 🏛 Lydford Gorge, Quarter mile

The **Castle Inn** is a distinguished hostelry dating from the middle of the 16th century. The two-room bar has a wealth of period detail including granite walls, slate floors, beamed ceilings and high-backed settles. Hogarth prints hang on the walls, and among the many curios is a collection of seven Lydford pennies minted during in the reign of Ethelred the Unready. In the restaurant is a great Saxon fireplace said to have come from the neighbouring Lydford Castle. Hosts Richard and Sarah Davies welcome visitors with a fine selection of cask ales and wines by the glass, and a choice of bar meals served lunchtime and evening and à la carte and table d'hote menus served every evening in the candlelit restaurant. Lydford is definitely a place for lingering, and the Castle Inn offers comfort and character in its eight en suite letting bedrooms, which range from a compact single to a four-poster and a de luxe room with its own roof garden.

15 The Chichester Arms

Chillaton, Lifton, Devon PL16 0HR
Tel: 01822 860283

Real Ales, Bar Food, Restaurant Menu,
No Smoking Area, Disabled Facilities

16 The Chipshop Inn

Tavistock, Devon PL19 8NT
Tel: 01822 832322

Real Ales, Bar Food

17 Clovelly Inn

Bratton Clovelly, Okehampton, Devon EX20 4JZ
Tel: 01837 871447

Real Ales, Bar Food, Restaurant Menu,
No Smoking Area

18 The Cornish Arms

15 West St, Tavistock, Devon PL19 8AN
Tel: 01822 612145

Real Ales, Bar Food, Restaurant Menu,
No Smoking Area, Disabled Facilities

19 The Crossways Inn

Folly Gate, Okehampton, Devon EX20 3AH
Tel: 01837 52088

Real Ales, Bar Food, Restaurant Menu,
No Smoking Area, Disabled Facilities

See panel opposite

20 Crown & Sceptre

Fore St, Holsworthy, Devon EX22 6EB
Tel: 01409 253645

Real Ales, Bar Food, Restaurant Menu,
No Smoking Area, Disabled Facilities

19 The Crossways Inn

Folly Gate, nr Okehampton, Devon EX20 3AH
☎ 01837 52088

Real Ales, Bar Food, Restaurant Menu,
No Smoking Area, Disabled Facilities

☛ On the A386 in Folly Gate, 2 miles N of
  Okehampton

🍺 Tinners and guests

🍴 11.30-3.30 & 6-9.30

⚓ Garden, car park

💳 Major cards except Amex

🕐 11-3 & 6-11

🏛 Okehampton 2 miles, Dartmoor 3 miles, Yes
  Tor 5 miles

John and Wendy Williams are the friendly
hosts at the **Crossways Inn,**, which they run
with the help of son Thomas and daughter
Amanda. Low beamed ceilings, panelling, small-
paned windows and a wood-burning stove
create a delightful ambience in the bar, where
three real ales are always on tap. Wendy is in
charge in the kitchen, which produces a good
variety of pub and restaurant classics.

21 The Dartmoor Inn

Merrivale, Princetown, Yelverton,
Devon PL20 6ST
Tel: 01822 890340

Real Ales, Bar Food, Restaurant Menu,
Accommodation, No Smoking Area,
Disabled Facilities

22 Devils Stone Inn

Shebbear, Beaworthy, Devon EX21 5RU
Tel: 01409 281210

Real Ales, Bar Food, Restaurant Menu,
Accommodation, No Smoking Area,
Disabled Facilities

23 Duke Of York

Iddesleigh, Winkleigh, Devon EX19 8BG
Tel: 01837 810253

Real Ales, Bar Food, Restaurant Menu,
Accommodation, Disabled Facilities

24 Elephant's Nest Inn

Horndon, Mary Tavy, Tavistock,
Devon PL19 9NQ
Tel: 01822 810273

Real Ales, Bar Food, Restaurant Menu,
No Smoking Area

25 Exeter Arms

East St, Okehampton, Devon EX20 1AS
Tel: 01837 53337

Disabled Facilities

26 Fountain Hotel

Fore St, Okehampton, Devon EX20 1AP
Tel: 01837 53900

Real Ales, Bar Food, Restaurant Menu,
Accommodation, No Smoking Area

27 Fox & Hounds Hotel

Bridestowe, Okehampton, Devon EX20 4HF
Tel: 01822 820206

Real Ales, Bar Food, Restaurant Menu,
Accommodation, No Smoking Area

28 George Hotel

5 Market St, Hatherleigh, Okehampton,
Devon EX20 3JN
Tel: 01837 810454

Real Ales, Bar Food, Restaurant Menu,
Accommodation, No Smoking Area

29 The Globe Inn

Beaford, Winkleigh, Devon EX19 8LR
Tel: 01805 603261

30 The Golden Fleece

Bodmin St, Holsworthy, Devon EX22 6BB
Tel: 01409 253263

Real Ales, Bar Food, Accommodation,
Disabled Facilities

31 The Golden Inn

Highampton, Beaworthy, Devon EX21 5LT
Tel: 01409 231200

Real Ales, Bar Food, Restaurant Menu,
No Smoking Area, Disabled Facilities

32 The Golden Lion
Clifton Rd, Exeter, Devon EX20 8XU
Tel: 01392 660068

Real Ales

33 The Green Dragon
Fore St, Langtree, Torrington, Devon EX38 8NG
Tel: 01805 601342

Real Ales, Bar Food, Restaurant Menu,
No Smoking Area, Disabled Facilities

34 The Green Dragon Inn
Northlew, Okehampton, Devon EX20 3NN
Tel: 01409 221228

Real Ales

35 H A Coombs
19 Brook St, Tavistock, Devon PL19 0HD
Tel: 01822 615736

Real Ales, Bar Food, Accommodation,
Disabled Facilities

36 Half Moon Inn
The Square, Sheepwash, Beaworthy,
Devon EX21 5NE
Tel: 01409 231376

Real Ales, Bar Food, Accommodation,
No Smoking Area, Disabled Facilities

37 The Harris Arms
Lewdown, Okehampton, Devon EX20 4PZ
Tel: 01566 783331

Real Ales, Restaurant Menu, No Smoking Area,
Disabled Facilities

38 The Highwayman Inn
Sourton, Okehampton, Devon EX20 4HN
Tel: 01837 861243

Real Ales, Bar Food, Accommodation,
No Smoking Area

39 Hotel Ensleigh
Endsleigh House, Milton Abbot, Tavistock,
Devon PL19 0PQ
Tel: 01822 870248

Restaurant Menu, Accommodation,
No Smoking Area

40 Junction Inn
Halwill Junction, Beaworthy, Devon EX21 5XR
Tel: 01409 221239

Real Ales, Bar Food, Restaurant Menu,
Disabled Facilities

41 The Kings Arms
St James St, Okehampton, Devon EX20 1DW
Tel: 01837 52809

Real Ales

42 Kings Arms Hotel
The Square, Holsworthy, Devon EX22 6DL
Tel: 01409 253517

Real Ales, Bar Food, Restaurant Menu,
Accommodation, No Smoking Area

43 The Laurels Inn
Petrockstowe, Okehampton, Devon EX20 3HJ
Tel: 01837 810578

Real Ales

44 Lewtrenchard Manor
Lewdown, Okehampton, Devon EX20 4PN
Tel: 01566 783256

Restaurant Menu, Accommodation,
No Smoking Area, Disabled Facilities

45 The Malt Scoop Inn
Merton, Okehampton, Devon EX20 3EA
Tel: 01805 603260

Real Ales, Bar Food

46 Mary Tavy Inn
Lane Head, Mary Tavy, Tavistock,
Devon PL19 9PN
Tel: 01822 810326

Real Ales, Bar Food, Restaurant Menu,
No Smoking Area

47 Molesworth Arms
Pyworthy, Holsworthy, Devon EX22 6SU
Tel: 01409 254669

Real Ales, Bar Food, Restaurant Menu,
No Smoking Area

48 Moor View House

Vale Down, Lydford, Okehampton,
Devon EX20 4BB
Tel: 01822 820220

Restaurant Menu, Accommodation,
No Smoking Area

49 The Old Union Inn

Stibb Cross, Torrington, Devon EX38 8LH
Tel: 01805 601253

Real Ales, Bar Food, Restaurant Menu,
Accommodation, No Smoking Area,
Disabled Facilities

50 Olde Market Inn

Chapel St, Holsworthy, Devon EX22 6AY
Tel: 01409 253941

Bar Food, Restaurant Menu, No Smoking Area,
Disabled Facilities

51 Ordulph Arms

Kilworthy Hill, Tavistock, Devon PL19 0AW
Tel: 01822 615048

Real Ales, Bar Food, Restaurant Menu

52 Peter Tavy Inn

Peter Tavy, Tavistock, Devon PL19 9NN
Tel: 01822 810348

Real Ales, Bar Food, Restaurant Menu,
No Smoking Area

See panel below

53 Plume Of Feathers Hotel

38 Fore St, Okehampton, Devon EX20 1HB
Tel: 01837 52815

Real Ales, Bar Food

54 Plymouth Inn

26 West St, Okehampton, Devon EX20 1HH
Tel: 01837 53633

Real Ales, Bar Food, Restaurant Menu

See panel on page 33

---

52 Peter Tavy Inn

Peter Tavy, nr Tavistock, Devon PL19 9NN
☎ 01822 810348

**Real Ales, Bar Food, Restaurant Menu,
No Smoking Area**

- ☞ Off the A386 3 miles NE of Tavistock
- 🍺 Princetown Brewery ales, Sharps Doom Bar
- 🍴 12-2 & 6.30-9
- 🅿 Car park, garden
- 💳 All the major cards
- 🏆 Top recommendations in leading food guides
- 🕐 12-3 & 6-11 (Sun to 10.30)
- 🏛 Tavistock 3 miles, Wheal Betsy Pumping Engine House 1 mile

Few inns anywhere in the land enjoy the reputation earned by the renowned **Peter Tavy Inn**, which draws visitors from near and far with its delightful setting, cheerful atmosphere and superb food and drink. Booking is recommended every session in the restaurant, where the blackboard menus offer a fantastic choice of dishes cooked by one of the most talented teams in the country. Some dishes are staunchly British, while others reflect worldwide influences, and the award-winning food is complemented by a good choice of wines by glass or bottle; other drinks include well-kept real ales, local farm cider and 30 malts. When the weather is kind the picnic benches in the garden are in great demand, but inside or out, rain or shine, a visit to this outstanding inn is an occasion to savour.

60 Tally Ho

Market Street, Hatherleigh, Devon EX20 3JN

☎ 01837 810306   🌐 www.hatherleigh.org.uk

Real Ales, Bar Food, Restaurant Menu,
Accommodation, No Smoking Area,
Disabled Facilities

- In Hatherleigh, 6 miles NW of Okehampton off the A386
- Good choice from local breweries
- 12-2 & 6.15-9
- 3 en suite rooms
- Garden
- Major cards accepted
- 11-11 (Sun 12-10.30)
- Okehampton 6 miles, Dartmoor 7 miles

Hatherleigh is a medieval market town in the heart of rural Devon, with a very well-preserved 15th century church set high above the Lew Valley. It also has an outstanding pub on Market Street, where the Tuesday market has been held for many centuries. Ady Taylor, in the licensed trade for 17 years, runs the Tally Ho with Marion, Neil and Adele, and together they make a fine team at this atmospheric inn.

The oldest parts date back to the 15th century and there's a delightful old-world look and feel throughout, with gnarled timbers and beams, log fires, ornaments and memorabilia of days gone by. The inn also has a really lovely sheltered beer garden with a barbecue area. The three real ales – details chalked up on a board above the bar counter- all come from local breweries, and hungry

visitors can take their pick from either bar or restaurant menus. Most of the produce is sourced locally, and some comes from the inn's own garden, grown without pesticides or fertilisers. Food can be eaten anywhere, but the little non-smoking restaurant has only 16 covers, so booking is a good idea,

particularly on Friday and Saturday. Meals are a delight from beginning to end, with a large selection of home-made desserts rounding things off in style.

The Tally Ho is definitely a place to savour, to relax and unwind, and Hatherleigh and the surrounding area are well worth taking time to explore. The inn has three en suite rooms (one with bath, two with showers) available on Bed & Breakfast terms all year round. This is good walking country – long stretches of the old track bed of the Okehampton-Bude railway provides attractive and reasonably level walking – and there's good fishing on the nearby River Torridge. The Tarka Trail Information Point is at Hatherleigh Pottery.

54 The Plymouth Inn

26 West Street, Okehampton, Devon EX20 1HH
☎ 01837 53655 🌐 www.theplymouthinn.org

Real Ales, Bar Food, Restaurant Menu

- ☛ On the edge of Okehampton
- 🍺 Skinners + 3 others
- 🍴 Lunchtime and evening (Bar & Restaurant)
- 🎵 Beer Festivals May and November
- ⛺ Garden
- 💳 Major cards except Amex & Diners
- 🕐 Open all day from 11am (12 noon Sunday)
- 🏛 Okehampton Castle 2 miles, Dartmoor Railway 1 mile, Dartmoor National Park 2 miles

A happy, relaxed atmosphere is generated in The Plymouth Inn. Four cask ales are always on tap; and many more during the beer festivals held here in May and November. The inn serves good-value home-cooked dishes, including four roasts for Sunday lunch.

55 Pretoria Vaults

22 North St, Okehampton, Devon EX20 1AR
Tel: 01837 52200

Real Ales

56 The Rams Head Inn

South St, Dolton, Winkleigh, Devon EX19 8QS
Tel: 01805 804255

Real Ales, Bar Food, Restaurant Menu,
Accommodation, No Smoking Area,
Disabled Facilities

57 Royal Inn

Horsebridge, Tavistock, Devon PL19 8PJ
Tel: 01822 870214

Real Ales, Bar Food, Restaurant Menu,
No Smoking Area, Disabled Facilities

See panel below

57 The Royal Inn

Horsebridge, Nr Tavistock, Devon PL19 8PJ
☎ 01822870214 🌐 www.royalinn.co.uk

**Real Ales, Bar Food, Restaurant Menu,
No Smoking Area, Disabled Facilities**

- ☛ Horsebridge lies off the A384 Tavistock-Launceston road
- 🍺 Skinners, East Street (Burnham-on-Sea)
- 🍴 12-2 & 6.30-9
- 🎵 Bar billiards, cribbage, dominoes
- ⛺ Garden, terrace, car park
- 💳 Major cards except Amex
- 🕐 12-3 & 6.30-11
- 🏛 Tavistock 5 miles, Launceston 10 miles

The Royal Inn is a very attractive white-painted building made even more appealing by surrounding trees and shrubs and a traditional red telephone box for a neighbour. The 15th century inn enjoys a scenic setting on an old drovers road, and was called the Pack Horse until the reign of Charles I. Behind the immaculate exterior, the bar is a very cosy, convivial place for a chat and a pint of real ale (East Street from Burnham-on-Sea is an interesting choice), and outside are two quaint patio areas. The Royal is widely and rightly recommended for its food, and the menu always tempts with a mouthwatering choice based on the finest locally sourced ingredients. Signature dishes include scallops and steaks, but everything listed on the chalkboard reflects the skills of the talented team in the kitchen.

65 The Union Inn

Fore Street, Dolton, Devon EX19 8QH
☎ 01805 804633

Bar Food, Accommodation, No Smoking Area

☞ On the B3217, 1½ miles from the A3124 between Winkleigh and Great Torrington

🍺 St Austell Tribute + guest

🍴 12-2.30 & 7-9.30

🛏 3 rooms

⛱ Small outside seating area, off-road parking

💳 Major cards except Amex and Diners

🕐 Lunchtime and evening (all day Sat & Sun seasonal, closed Wed)

🏛 Winkleigh 6 miles, Great Torrington 8 miles

Built many centuries ago as a classic Devon long house, the **Union Inn** was reborn in its current role in 1855. This year therefore sees 150 years of hospitality at this outstanding place, and with owner Amanda Thomas personally running the show that tradition is being carried on in the best possible style. The lovely black-and-white exterior is made even lovelier in spring and summer by climbing plants and hanging baskets, and the promise of the outside is more than fulfilled within.

The convivial bar has a very appealing old-world look assisted by beams and horse brasses, ornamental plates, country furniture, period prints and rural artefacts. There are comfortable cushioned window seats and banquettes in the lounge/dining area, and an armchair by the fire is a delightfully homely touch. The inn can safely stake its claim as one of the best eating places in the area, and the chef uses local produce to prepare all the dishes on the premises. Diners can eat anywhere in the inn, but such is the popularity of the place that booking is recommended for all meals to be sure of a table in the 30-cover non-smoking restaurant. Most of the meat

comes from a top-notch local butchers, and steak with all the trimmings is a perennial favourite. Other popular dishes including seasonal specialities such as Game dishes, homemade pies and fish specialities, with homemade desserts to round things off in style.

Children are welcome until 9 o'clock. The Union is closed on Wednesdays. The countryside around Dolton is well worth taking time to explore, and the inn's three guest bedrooms, all en suite, one with a four-poster, provide a very pleasant, civilised base. Dolton itself has a fine village church with a font that dates back more than 1,000 years.

58 The Royal Oak Inn
The Square, Dolton, Winkleigh,
Devon EX19 8QF
Tel: 01805 804288

Real Ales, Bar Food, Restaurant Menu,
Accommodation, No Smoking Area,
Disabled Facilities

59 Royal Standard Inn
Mary Tavy, Tavistock, Devon PL19 9QB
Tel: 01822 810289

Real Ales, Bar Food, Restaurant Menu

60 The Tally Ho
14 Market St, Hatherleigh, Okehampton,
Devon EX20 3JN
Tel: 01837 810306

Real Ales, Bar Food, Restaurant Menu,
Accommodation, No Smoking Area,
Disabled Facilities

See panel on page 32

61 Torridge Inn
Broad St, Black Torrington, Beaworthy,
Devon EX21 5PT
Tel: 01409 231243

Real Ales, Bar Food, Restaurant Menu,
No Smoking Area

62 The Tors
Belstone, Okehampton, Devon EX20 1QZ
Tel: 01837 840689

Real Ales, Bar Food, Restaurant Menu,
Accommodation, No Smoking Area

63 Trout 'n' Tipple
Parkwood Rd, Tavistock, Devon PL19 0JS
Tel: 01822 618886

Real Ales, Bar Food, No Smoking Area,
Disabled Facilities

64 The Union Inn
King St, Tavistock, Devon PL19 0DS
Tel: 01822 613115

Real Ales, Bar Food, Restaurant Menu,
No Smoking Area

65 Union Inn
Fore St, Dolton, Winkleigh, Devon EX19 8QH
Tel: 01805 804633

Bar Food, Accommodation, No Smoking Area

See panel opposite

66 The Village Inn
Ashwater, Beaworthy, Devon EX21 5EY
Tel: 01409 211200

Real Ales, Bar Food, Restaurant Menu,
No Smoking Area, Disabled Facilities

67 White Hart Hotel
Fore St, Okehampton, Devon EX20 1HD
Tel: 01837 52730

Real Ales, Bar Food, Restaurant Menu,
Accommodation, No Smoking Area

68 White Hart Hotel
Fore St, Holsworthy, Devon EX22 6EB
Tel: 01409 253475

Real Ales, Bar Food, Restaurant Menu,
Accommodation, No Smoking Area,
Disabled Facilities

69 White Hart Inn
Fore St, Bridestowe, Okehampton,
Devon EX20 4EL
Tel: 01837 861318

Real Ales, Bar Food, Restaurant Menu,
Accommodation, No Smoking Area,
Disabled Facilities

70 Woodacott Arms
Woodacott, Holsworthy, Devon EX22 7BT
Tel: 01409 261358

Real Ales

Section 2

Section 4

Gunnislake

Princetown 46
48
50

35
64
22
23

Callington
St Cleer

29
32
62
7

Buckland
Monachorum 13

11
31
52
55
Yelverton

St Ive

Dobwalls
Liskeard
Pillaton

St Mellion
Bere Alston 66

16

38 58

45

65

Tideford
Saltash

3 26
49 51 1
56

33
21
37

Duloe
Trerulefoot

PLYMOUTH

18
6

40 9

Looe
Seaton

Torpoint

Plympton

20 61
Sparkwell
8
34

30 25
42 63

Porthallow
Polperro

Freathy
Kingsand

39

5 24 14 47 17
43 54 Hooe
59

4 2

19 Brixton
27 53

Rame

41 28 44
15
Wembury
Newton
Ferrers

12
57
60

10
36

II Pub or Inn Reference Number - Detailed Information

12 Pub or Inn Reference Number - Summary Entry

⬤ ◼ Place of interest mentioned in the chapter introduction

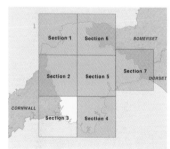

Section 1 | Section 6 | SOMERSET

Section 2 | Section 5 | Section 7 | DORSET

CORNWALL | Section 3 | Section 4

PLYMOUTH & DISTRICT

Plymouth became the main base of the British Navy in the 16th century and the seafaring connection remains strong. At Plympton, now more or less a suburb of Plymouth, Saltram House is one of the county's grandest mansions.

Bere Alston

Upstream from this village southwest of Tavistock is one of the country's most popular visitor attractions – **Morwellham Quay**, a historic port, copper mine, preserved Victorian village and open-air museum. One of the ships that transported copper ore has been restored to its original condition.

Buckland Monachorum

Tucked away in a secluded valley, **Buckland Abbey** was founded in 1278 and became an influential Cistercian monastery. It is best known as the last home of Sir Francis Drake, and among the many memorabilia on display is Drake's Drum, which according to legend will sound whenever the realm of England is in peril. Between Buckland

Monachorum and Crapstone, the **Garden House** is centred on an enchanting walled garden around the romantic ruins of a medieval vicarage.

Plymouth

It was Plymouth Hoe, overlooking Plymouth Sound, that in 1588 the Commander of the Fleet, Sir Francis Drake, was playing bowls when he was informed of the approach of the Spanish Armada. The influence of Drake and the sea are in strong evidence here, from the **Citadel** and the **Mayflower Stone** to the **National Marine Aquarium**. Many of the city's interesting old buildings are in and around the Barbican. Visitors can discover the colourful history of gin at **Black Friars Distillery**, the working home of Plymouth Gin since 1793.

Plympton

Plympton is home to one of Devon's grandest mansions, **Saltram House**, built in the 18th century round a Tudor core. The magnificent Robert Adam-designed State Rooms are filled with beautiful things, and the lovely grounds run down to the Plym estuary. From the village, the **Plym Valley Railway** carries passengers in rolling stock from the 1950s and 1960s on a restored part of the GWR to the

Buckland Abbey

The Hoe, Plymouth

local beauty spot of Plym Bridge.

Princetown

In the heart of Dartmoor, some 1,400 feet above sea level, this isolated settlement is the location of **Dartmoor Prison** and the **Moorland Visitor Centre**.

Sparkwell

Just north of Sparkwell lies the **Dartmoor Wildlife Park**, home to the largest

collection of Big Cats in the Southwest and many other carnivores. Also on the site is the **Falconry Centre** with a large collection of birds of prey and regular flying displays.

Yelverton

This sizeable village on the very edge of Dartmoor is home to the **Yelverton Paperweight Centre**, where a fascinating collection of some 800 glass paperweights has been assembled.

---

1 Abbots Way

Southway Drive, Plymouth, Devon PL6 6QW
Tel: 01752 774481
Real Ales, Bar Food

2 The Billacombe Tavern

Billacombe Rd, Plymouth, Devon PL9 7HG
Tel: 01752 407927
Real Ales, Bar Food, Restaurant Menu,
No Smoking Area

3 The Blue Bird Hotel

164 Eggbuckland Rd , Plymouth,
Devon PL5 4NH
Tel: 01752 774367
Real Ales, Bar Food, No Smoking Area

4 The Blue Peter

68 Pomphlett Rd, Plymstock, Plymouth,
Devon PL9 7BN
Tel: 01752 402255
Real Ales, Bar Food, No Smoking Area

5 Boringdon Arms
Boringdon Terrace, Turnchapel, Plymouth,
Devon PL9 9TQ
Tel: 01752 402053

Real Ales, Bar Food, Restaurant Menu,
Accommodation, No Smoking Area

6 Boringdon Hall Hotel
Boringdon Hill, Colebrook, Plympton,
Devon PL7 4DP
Tel: 01752 344455

Bar Food, Restaurant Menu, Accommodation,
No Smoking Area

7 The Burrator Inn
Dousland, Yelverton, Devon PL20 6NP
Tel: 01822 853121

Real Ales, Bar Food, Accommodation,
No Smoking Area, Disabled Facilities

8 Chaddlewood Inn
100 Glen Rd, Plympton, Plymouth,
Devon PL7 2XS
Tel: 01752 349951

Real Ales, Bar Food, No Smoking Area,
Disabled Facilities

9 The Cornwood Inn
Cornwood, Ivybridge, Devon PL21 9PU
Tel: 01752 837225

Real Ales, Bar Food, Restaurant Menu,
No Smoking Area

10 Dartmoor Union Inn
Fore St, Holbeton, Plymouth, Devon PL8 1NE
Tel: 01752 830288

Real Ales, Bar Food, Restaurant Menu,
No Smoking Area

11 Devon Tors Bar
Yelverton, Devon PL20 6DW
Tel: 01822 853604

Real Ales, Bar Food, Restaurant Menu,
No Smoking Area

12 The Dolphin Inn
Riverside Rd East, Newton Ferrers, Plymouth,
Devon PL8 1AE
Tel: 01752 872007

Real Ales, Bar Food, Restaurant Menu,
No Smoking Area

13 Drake Manor Inn
The Village, Buckland Monachorum, Yelverton,
Devon PL20 7NA
Tel: 01822 853892

Real Ales, Bar Food, Restaurant Menu,
No Smoking Area

14 Drakes Drum
19 Radford Park Rd, Plymstock, Plymouth,
Devon PL9 9DN
Tel: 01752 402613

Real Ales, Bar Food, Restaurant Menu,
No Smoking Area

15 Eddystone Inn
Heybrook Drive, Heybrook Bay, Plymouth,
Devon PL9 0BN
Tel: 01752 862356

Real Ales, Bar Food, Restaurant Menu,
No Smoking Area

16 Edgcumbe Hotel
2 Fore St, Bere Alston, Yelverton,
Devon PL20 7AD
Tel: 01822 840252

Real Ales

17 Elburton Hotel
221 Elburton Rd, Elburton, Plymouth,
Devon PL9 8HX
Tel: 01752 403213

Real Ales, Bar Food, Restaurant Menu,
No Smoking Area

18 Elfordleigh Hotel
Plympton, Plymouth, Devon PL7 5EB
Tel: 01752 336428

Bar Food, Restaurant Menu, Accommodation,
Disabled Facilities

19 | The Foxhound Inn

Kingsbridge Road, Brixton, Devon PL8 2AH

☎ 01752 880271 | 🌐 www.foxhoundinn.co.uk

Bar Food, Restaurant Menu

☞ On the A379 Plymouth-Kingsbridge road 3 miles E of Plymouth

🍺 Local brews + Courage Best

🍴 12-2 & 6.30-9 (weekends 5.30-9.30)

🎵 Charity quiz 1 Wed a month, Jazz night 1 Wed a month

🅿 Car park

💳 Major cards except Amex and Diners

🕐 Lunchtime and evening, (Summer all day Fri, Sat & Sun

🏛 Plymouth 3 miles, Wembury 3 miles

Established as a pub in the late-18th century, the **Foxhound Inn** has been offering a warm welcome and friendly hospitality to locals and visitors alike ever since. The interior is delightfully comfortable and cosy, with traditional features such as exposed beams and open fires, photographs of customers and tenants, pictures, plates, ornamental copperware and a few nautical touches.

Pauline and Neil Bradley, who took over as leaseholders in November 2004, brought with them many years' experience in the licensed trade and hotel management, and they have lost no time in winning new friends while continuing to offer the attractions of a much-loved local to the many regulars who come here from Brixton and the neighbouring villages and who come here to get away from the bustle of Plymouth. Behind the stone-built whitewashed exterior the cosy, comfortable

bar is a perfect spot for enjoying a glass of one of the local brews or Courage Best

The Foxhound is also a great place for a snack or a meal. Most of the produce that goes into the kitchen is sourced locally, including fish bought daily from the Barbican

market and meat from the best butchers. The ever-changing menus cater brilliantly for all tastes: pub classics such as prawn cocktail, steak, ale & mushroom pie or braised lamb shanks; restaurant favourites like game terrine or chicken Caesar salad; and dishes inspired from afar such as Japanese-style king prawns with a sweet chilli dip, chicken or vegetable fajitas and beef teriyaki with noodles and a black bean and plum sauce. Whatever the route taken with the starters and main courses, many diners comeback to the West Country with delights like apple & blackberry crumble served with – what else – Devon clotted cream. On one Wednesday a month the pub hosts a charity quiz, and on another Wednesday there's a lively jazz session.

19 ## The Foxhound Inn

Brixton, Plymouth, Devon PL8 2AH
Tel: 01752 880271

Bar Food, Restaurant Menu

See panel opposite

20 ## The Garden Restaurant @ Miners Arms

Hemerdon, Plymouth, Devon PL7 5BU
Tel: 01752 336040

Real Ales, Bar Food, Restaurant Menu,
No Smoking Area

21 ## The George

399 Tavistock Rd, Plymouth, Devon PL6 7HB
Tel: 01752 771527

Bar Food, Restaurant Menu, No Smoking Area

22 ## The Halfway House Inn

Halfway House, Grenofen, Tavistock,
Devon PL19 9ER
Tel: 01822 612960

Real Ales, Bar Food, Restaurant Menu,
Accommodation, No Smoking Area,
Disabled Facilities

23 ## The Horn Of Plenty

Gulworthy, Tavistock, Devon PL19 8JD
Tel: 01822 832528

Real Ales, Restaurant Menu, Accommodation,
No Smoking Area

24 ## Hotel Mount Batten

Lawrence Rd, Mount Batten, Plymouth,
Devon PL9 9SJ
Tel: 01752 405500

Real Ales, Bar Food, Restaurant Menu,
Accommodation, Disabled Facilities

25 ## The Hunting Lodge

Ivybridge, Devon PL21 9JN
Tel: 01752 892409

Real Ales, Bar Food, Restaurant Menu,
No Smoking Area, Disabled Facilities

26 ## Kings Arms

Tamerton Foliot Rd, Plymouth, Devon PL5 4NH
Tel: 01752 773213

Real Ales, Bar Food, Restaurant Menu,
No Smoking Area, Disabled Facilities

27 ## Kitley House Hotel

Yealmpton, Plymouth, Devon PL8 2NW
Tel: 01752 881555

Bar Food, Restaurant Menu, Accommodation,
No Smoking Area, Disabled Facilities

28 ## Langdon Court

Down Thomas, Plymouth, Devon PL9 0DY
Tel: 01752 862358

Real Ales, Bar Food, Restaurant Menu,
Accommodation, No Smoking Area

29 ## Leaping Salmon

Whitchurch Rd, Horrabridge, Yelverton,
Devon PL20 7TP
Tel: 01822 852939

Real Ales, Bar Food, Restaurant Menu,
No Smoking Area

30 ## The Lee Mill Inn

Lee Mill, Ivybridge, Devon PL21 9EF
Tel: 01752 892394

Real Ales

31 ## Leg O' Mutton Inn

Leg O Mutton Corner, Yelverton,
Devon PL20 6AA
Tel: 01822 854195

Real Ales, Bar Food, Restaurant Menu,
No Smoking Area, Disabled Facilities

32 ## The London Inn

23 Station Rd, Horrabridge, Yelverton,
Devon PL20 7ST
Tel: 01822 853567

Real Ales, Bar Food, Restaurant Menu,
No Smoking Area

33 Lopes Arms

27-29 Tavistock Rd, Roborough, Plymouth, Devon
PL6 7BD
Tel: 01752 777299

Real Ales, Bar Food, Restaurant Menu,
Accommodation, No Smoking Area

34 Lyneham Inn

Plympton, Plymouth, Devon PL7 5AT
Tel: 01752 336955

Real Ales, Bar Food, Restaurant Menu,
No Smoking Area

35 The Market Inn

2 Whitchurch Rd, Tavistock, Devon PL19 9BB
Tel: 01822 613556

Real Ales, Bar Food, Restaurant Menu,
No Smoking Area

36 Mildmay Colours Inn

Fore St, Holbeton, Plymouth, Devon PL8 1NA
Tel: 01752 830248

Real Ales, Bar Food, Restaurant Menu,
Accommodation, No Smoking Area

37 Millstones Country Hotel

436-438 Tavistock Rd, Plymouth,
Devon PL6 7HQ
Tel: 01752 773734

Restaurant Menu, Accommodation,
No Smoking Area

38 Moorland Links Hotel

Yelverton, Devon PL20 6DA
Tel: 01822 852245

Real Ales, Bar Food, Restaurant Menu,
Accommodation, No Smoking Area,
Disabled Facilities

39 Morley Arms

4 Billacombe Rd, Laira Bridge, Plymouth,
Devon PL9 7HP
Tel: 01752 401191

Real Ales, Bar Food, Restaurant Menu,
No Smoking Area

40 The Mountain Inn

Lutton, Ivybridge, Devon PL21 9SA
Tel: 01752 837247

Real Ales, Bar Food, No Smoking Area

41 The Mussel Inn

Renny Rd, Down Thomas, Plymouth,
Devon PL9 0AQ
Tel: 01752 862238

Real Ales, Bar Food, Restaurant Menu,
Accommodation, No Smoking Area

42 The New Country Inn

Smithaleigh, Plymouth, Devon PL7 5AX
Tel: 01752 896555

Real Ales, Bar Food, Restaurant Menu,
Accommodation, No Smoking Area,
Disabled Facilities

See panel opposite

43 The New Inn

Boringdon Rd, Turnchapel, Plymouth,
Devon PL9 9TB
Tel: 01752 402765

Real Ales, Bar Food, Restaurant Menu,
Accommodation, No Smoking Area

44 The Odd Wheel

Knighton Rd, Wembury, Plymouth,
Devon PL9 0JD
Tel: 01752 862287

Real Ales, Restaurant Menu, No Smoking Area

45 The Olde Plough Inn

Bere Ferrers, Yelverton, Devon PL20 7JL
Tel: 01822 840358

Real Ales, Bar Food, Restaurant Menu,
No Smoking Area, Disabled Facilities

46 The Plume Of Feathers Inn

Plymouth Hill, Princetown, Yelverton,
Devon PL20 6QQ
Tel: 01822 890240

Real Ales, Bar Food, Restaurant Menu

42 The New County Inn & Smithaleigh Hotel

Smithaleigh, nr Plympton, Plymouth,
Devon PL7 5AX

☎ 01752 896555 🌐 www.thenewcountyinn.co.uk

Real Ales, Bar Food, Restaurant Menu, Accommodation, No Smoking Area, Disabled Facilities

- Off the A38 from Woodland or Plympton on a minor road through Lee Mill to Smithaleigh
- Courage
- Lunchtime and evening
- 25 en suite rooms
- Garden, patio, car park
- Major cards accepted
- Lunchtime and evening
- Plympton 3 miles, Plymouth 4 miles, Ivybridge 3 miles

In a little village in the beautiful South Hams countryside, the New Country Inn & Smithaleigh Hotel combines the best features of inn, hotel, restaurant and function venue. It's run by licensees Diane and Julie, who are reinforcing the inn's reputation for good food, quality accommodation and friendly, thoughtful service. The inn serves a good selection of beers and wines, and excellent home-cooked dishes that extend from classics like beer-battered fish and steak & ale pie to warm crispy duck salad with plum sauce, Cajun pasta and medallions of monkfish with wilted greens and a tomato & mango salsa. The 25 well-appointed en suite guest bedrooms – twins, doubles, family rooms and two honeymoon four-posters – are situated in a converted farmhouse and round a courtyard. The setting, in colourful gardens and grounds, makes this a popular venue for special occasions, and up to 150 guests can be seated in the function room.

47 The Plymstock Inn

88 Church Rd, Plymstock, Plymouth,
Devon PL9 9BD
Tel: 01752 482777

Real Ales, Bar Food, Restaurant Menu, No Smoking Area, Disabled Facilities

48 Prince Of Wales Hotel

Tavistock Rd, Princetown, Yeiverton,
Devon PL20 6QF
Tel: 01822 890219

Real Ales, Bar Food, Restaurant Menu, Accommodation, No Smoking Area

49 The Queens Arms

Seven Stars Lane, Tamerton Foliot, Plymouth, Devon
PL5 4NN
Tel: 01752 772693

Real Ales

50 The Railway Inn

Princetown, Yelverton, Devon PL20 6QT
Tel: 01822 890232

Real Ales, Bar Food, Accommodation, No Smoking Area

51 Rising Sun Inn

138 Eggbuckland Rd, Plymouth,
Devon PL5 4NH
Tel: 01752 774359

Real Ales, Bar Food, Restaurant Menu

52 The Rock Inn

Yelverton, Devon PL20 6DS
Tel: 01822 852022

Real Ales, Bar Food, Restaurant Menu, No Smoking Area, Disabled Facilities

58 | The Skylark Inn

Clearbrook, nr Yelverton, Devon PL20 6JD
☎ 01822 853258   🌐 www.theskylarkinn.co.uk

Real Ales, Bar Food, Restaurant Menu

- 🏴 Yelverton stands off the A386 4 miles N of Plymouth
- 🍺 Otter, Sharps, Courage
- 🍴 12-2 & 6-9
- ⛴ Garden, car park
- 💳 Major cards accepted
- 🕐 11-11 (Sun 12-10.30) in summer; L & D Mon-Fri and all day Sat & Sun in winter
- 🏛 Dartmoor on the doorstep; Buckland Abbey 3 miles, Plymouth 4 miles

The **Skylark** is a truly outstanding inn located in the village of Clearbrook, a short drive from Yelverton and a mile or so off the A386 Tavistock-Plymouth road. Lying within the Dartmoor National Park, it provides an ideal refreshment stop for walkers, cyclists and motorists touring the area. It is also a popular 'local', and everyone appreciates the warm welcome from leaseholder Victor Guerrero and the charming old-world ambience. The bar keeps four real ales on tap – Otter, Sharpe's Special, Courage Best and a regularly changing guest. A selection of good-quality food is served lunchtime and evening Monday to Saturday and from 12 to 9 on Sunday. The choice runs from baguettes, jacket potatoes and salads to meat, fish, pasta and vegetarian main courses and a tempting list of home-made desserts. Children are welcome in the non-smoking family room at the rear.

64 | The Whitchurch Inn

Church Hill, Whitchurch, nr Tavistock, Devon PL19 9ED
☎ 01822 612181   🌐 www.thewhitechurchinn.co.uk

Real Ales, Bar Food, Restaurant Menu, No Smoking Area

- 🏴 A short drive S of Tavistock on the A386
- 🍺 London Pride, Jail Ale, Bass
- 🍴 12-2.30 & 6.30-9.45 (all day Sat & Sun)
- 💳 Major cards except Amex
- 🕐 12-11
- 🏛 Tavistock 1 mile, Dartmoor Forest, The Garden House 1 mile, Morwellham Quay 2 miles, Buckland Abbey 3 miles

Traditional features and contemporary style and comfort combine at the **Whitchurch Inn**, which stands by the church in a pleasant village on the edge of Dartmoor. This splendid free house has been managed since 1999 by Rachel Newphry, who, with her hardworking staff, offers warm hospitality and excellent, friendly service. Four real ales are always available in the bar, where the traditional features include darkwood furniture, stone walls, a log-burning stove, copper and brass, old prints and beams thought to have been fashioned from ship's timbers. Food is served lunchtime and evening and all day Saturday and Sunday; the choice runs from bar snacks to full meals, with something for all tastes and appetites. Booking is advisable to be sure of a table at the weekend.

53 The Rose & Crown
Market St, Yealmpton, Plymouth, Devon PL8 2EB
Tel: 01752 880223

Real Ales, Bar Food, Restaurant Menu,
No Smoking Area, Disabled Facilities

54 Royal Oak
Lake Rd, Plymouth, Devon PL9 9QY
Tel: 01752 512900

Real Ales, Bar Food, Restaurant Menu

55 Royal Oak Inn
Meavy, Yelverton, Devon PL20 6PJ
Tel: 01822 852944

Real Ales, Bar Food, Restaurant Menu,
No Smoking Area

56 Seven Stars Inn
Seven Stars Lane, Tamerton Foliot, Plymouth, Devon
PL5 4NN
Tel: 01752 772901

Real Ales, Bar Food, Restaurant Menu,
No Smoking Area, Disabled Facilities

57 The Ship Inn
Noss Mayo, Plymouth, Devon PL8 1EW
Tel: 01752 872387

Real Ales, Bar Food, Restaurant Menu,
No Smoking Area, Disabled Facilities

58 The Skylark Inn
Clearbrook, Yelverton, Devon PL20 6JD
Tel: 01822 853258

Real Ales, Bar Food, Restaurant Menu

See panel opposite

59 The Staddy
144 Staddiscombe Rd, Staddiscombe, Plymouth,
Devon PL9 9LT
Tel: 01752 401144

Bar Food

60 The Swan Inn
Noss Mayo, Plymouth, Devon PL8 1EE
Tel: 01752 872392

Real Ales, Bar Food, Restaurant Menu,
No Smoking Area

61 The Treby Arms
Sparkwell, Plymouth, Devon PL7 5DD
Tel: 01752 837363

Bar Food, Restaurant Menu

62 The Walkhampton Inn
Walkhampton, Yelverton, Devon PL20 6JY
Tel: 01822 855556

Real Ales, Bar Food, Restaurant Menu,
No Smoking Area

63 Westward Inn
Lee Mill Bridge, Ivybridge, Devon PL21 9EE
Tel: 01752 892626

Real Ales, Bar Food, Restaurant Menu,
No Smoking Area, Disabled Facilities

64 The Whitchurch
Church Hill, Whitchurch, Tavistock,
Devon PL19 9ED
Tel: 01822 612181

Real Ales, Bar Food, Restaurant Menu,
No Smoking Area

See panel oppopsite

65 The White Thorn
Shaugh Prior, Plymouth, Devon PL7 5HA
Tel: 01752 839245

Real Ales, Bar Food, Disabled Facilities

66 Who'd Have Thought It
Milton Combe, Yelverton, Devon PL20 6HP
Tel: 01822 853313

Real Ales, Bar Food, Restaurant Menu,
No Smoking Area

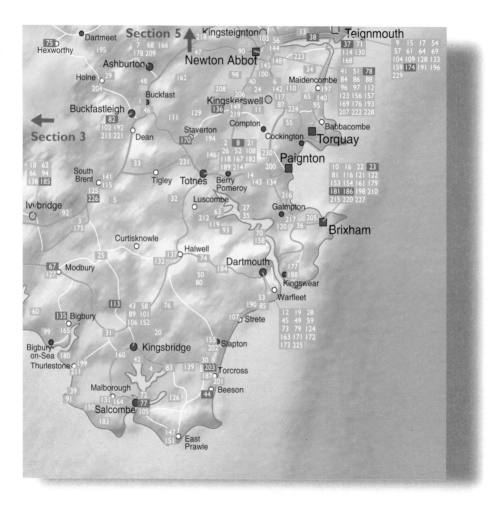

Section 5

Kingsteignton
Dartmeet
Hexworthy
7 68 166
178 209
195
Ashburton
Holne 29
Buckfast
Buckfastleigh
102 192
213 221
Section 3
Dean
Staverton
Compton
Cockington
Torquay
Paignton
South Brent
Tigley Totnes Berry Pomeroy
Luscombe
Galmpton
Ivybridge
Curtisknowle
Halwell
Brixham
Modbury
Dartmouth
Kingswear
Warfleet
Bigbury
Strete
Bigbury-on-Sea
Thurlestone
Kingsbridge
Slapton
Torcross
Malborough
Beeson
Salcombe
East Prawle

Teignmouth

Newton Abbot

Maidencombe

Kingskerswell

Babbacombe

Teignmouth

Kingsteignton
Newton Abbot
Maidencombe
Kingskerswell
Babbacombe
Torquay
Paignton
Brixham

	Pub or Inn Reference Number - Detailed Information
	Pub or Inn Reference Number - Summary Entry
●■	Place of interest mentioned in the chapter introduction

Section 1 | Section 6 | SOMERSET

Section 2 | Section 5 | Section 7 | DORSET

CORNWALL | Section 3 | Section 4

TORBAY AND THE SOUTH HAMS

The great sweep of Tor Bay contains the popular resorts of Torquay, Paignton and Brixham. Further down the coast is the town of Dartmouth with its strong naval connections, while at the southern edge lies the beautiful area known as the South Hams, with a wide variety of landscapes and seascapes.

Ashburton

An appealing little town just inside Dartmoor National Park; it became one of Devon's four stannary towns in 1305. The cloth industry later took over from tin mining as the major employer, and both legacies are explored in the **Ashburton Museum**. Here, too, can be seen old farming implements, Victorian toys, local minerals and a collection of North American Indian artefacts.

Berry Pomeroy

Reputed to be the most haunted castle in

Burgh Island and Bigbury

Devon, **Berry Pomeroy Castle** is also the most romantic, and its position on a wooded hillside overlooking the beautiful Gatcombe Valley gives the ruins a wonderfully tranquil air.

Bigbury-on-Sea/Burgh Island

Just off the shore of the popular resort of Bigbury-on-Sea is Burgh Island, an island only at high tide. The extravagant **Art Deco Hotel** on the island has attracted many distinguished visitors down the years, including Noël Coward, Agatha Christie and the Duke of Windsor and Mrs Wallis Simpson. The island's **Pilchard Inn** dates from the 14th century.

Brixham

The most southerly of the three towns that make up the great Torbay conurbation is an important fishing town and a popular sailing and holiday resort. Brixham's little lighthouse makes up for its lack of height (just 15 feet) by standing on the 200ft cliffs within **Berry Head Country Park**.

Buckfast

Buckfast Abbey, on the edge of Dartmoor, was founded as a Benedictine monastery in the 11th century. The Abbey was closed by Henry VIII, but in 1882 the present community of monks returned and began to rebuild their home on the medieval foundations. The Abbey Church, completed in 1938, is the centrepiece of the site, which also includes the monastic produce shop, a physic garden and the National Lavender Collection.

Buckfastleigh

Buckfastleigh is the western terminus and headquarters of the **South Devon Railway**, on which steam-hauled trains run on a beautiful 7-mile branch line along the River Dart to Staverton and Totnes.

Cockington

A mile or so from the centre of Torquay, Cockington is a picturesque rural oasis of thatched cottages, a working forge and an inn designed by Lutyens. From the inn there is a pleasant walk to **Cockington Court**, a stately old manor house that is now a craft centre and gallery.

Compton

Compton Castle is a wonderful fortified manor house that dates back to the 14th century. Complete with battlements, towers, a portcullis and an impressive Great Hall, the Gilbert family's ancestral home is in the care of the National Trust.

Dartmeet

Dartmeet lies at a famous beauty spot where the East and West Dart rivers meet in a steep wooded valley. At their junction is the single-span **Clapper Bridge** dating from the 15th century. The **Dart Valley Nature Reserve** is the largest of Devon Wildlife Trust's reserves and also one of the most spectacular.

Dartmouth

For centuries this delightful little town was one of the country's principal ports, and the maritime connection is shown in the **Britannia Royal Naval College** and its museum. **Dartmouth Castle**, which guards the entrance to the Dart Estuary,

Dartmouth Castle

was built by Edward IV after the War of the Roses. Dartmouth's railway station is interesting in that it has never seen a train. It was built by the Great Western Railway as the terminus of their line from Torbay but the line actually ended at Kingswear and passengers completed their journey to Dartmouth on the GWR ferry.

Galmpton

Close to this village southwest of Torquay is the National Trust's **Greenway**, the birthplace of the navigator Sir Humphrey Gilbert and the home of Agatha Christie for the last 30 years of her life. The glorious gardens are open to the public on certain days in the summer.

Kingsbridge

The **Shambles**, an Elizabethan market arcade, is a reminder that Kingsbridge was once an important market centre serving the surrounding towns and villages. Beyond the Church of St Edmund is the **Cookworthy Museum**, where visitors can learn about the town's history and look in on a 17th century school room, a Victorian kitchen and an Edwardian pharmacy.

Kingswear

Kingswear is the terminus of the **Paignton and Dartmouth Steam Railway**, and from here passengers can take the 10-minute ferry ride to Dartmouth. Above the estuary stand the imposing remains of **Kingswear Castle**, while to the northwest of the town lies **Coleton Fishacre House and Gardens**, designed in the 1920s for Rupert and Dorothy d'Oyly Carte of Gilbert & Sullivan fame.

Newton Abbot

An ancient market town where in 1688 William, Prince of orange, was proclaimed King William III. **Newton Abbot Museum** offers a glimpse into the past of this historic town, and among other places well worth a visit are **Tucker's Maltings**, a traditional malthouse open to the public, and the National Trust's **Bradley Manor**, a small manor house dating mainly from around 1420. **Newton Abbot Racecourse** stages National Hunt races from the autumn through to the spring.

Paignton

A near neighbour of Torquay, with two superb beaches, a pier and a promenade. The town's most interesting building is the exuberant **Oldway Mansion**, built in 1874 for the sewing machine manufacturer Isaac Singer. **Paignton Zoo** is the main family attraction, and another experience not to be missed is a trip on the **Paignton and Dartmouth Steam Railway**.

Salcombe

In a beautiful setting at the mouth of the Kingsbridge Estuary, Salcombe is a favoured sailing centre, and small fishing fleet still operates from Batson Creek. To the south lies **Overbecks**, a charming Edwardian house set in lovely sheltered gardens. Displays in the Museum include late-Victorian photographs of the area, shipbuilding tools, model boats and toys.

Slapton

Slapton Ley is Devon's largest natural freshwater lake; the shallow lake and the land around it is designated a Site of Special

Torquay

born here in 1890, and the **Agatha Christie Memorial Room** in Torre Abbey contains a wonderful, personal collection of Agatha Christie memorabilia. An exhibition of photographs records her life in **Torquay Museum**, whose treasures also includes animal bones and other items discovered at nearby Kents Cavern.

Scientific Interest and also a nature reserve that is home to a large number of freshwater fish, insects, water-loving plants and native and migrating birds. An associated sturdy centre is located in the village.

Torquay

The premier resort of southwest England, Torquay enjoyed royal patronage from its early days. Agatha Miller (later Christie) was

Totnes

The impressive remains of **Totnes Castle** include what is generally recognised as the best-preserved motte and bailey castles in Devon. The town **Museum** and the **Devonshire Collection of Period Costume** are both well worth a visit, as is **Totnes Town Mill**, a restored waterwheel and mill. Totnes is at one end of the **South Devon Railway** that runs by the River Dart to Staverton and Buckfastleigh.

1 Abbey Inn
30 Buckfast Rd, Buckfast, Buckfastleigh,
Devon TQ11 0EA
Tel: 01364 642343

Real Ales, Bar Food, Restaurant Menu,
Accommodation, No Smoking Area

2 The Albert Inn
32 Bridgetown, Totnes, Devon TQ9 5AD
Tel: 01803 863214

Real Ales, Bar Food

3 Anchor Inn
1 Lutterburn St, Ugborough, Ivybridge,
Devon PL21 0NG
Tel: 01752 892283

Real Ales, Bar Food, Restaurant Menu,
No Smoking Area

4 Ashburton Arms
West Charleton, Kingsbridge, Devon TQ7 2AH
Tel: 01548 531242

Real Ales, Bar Food, Restaurant Menu,
No Smoking Area

5 The Avon Inn
Avonwick, South Brent, Devon TQ10 9NB
Tel: 01364 73475

Real Ales, Bar Food, Restaurant Menu,
No Smoking Area

6 The Barn Owl Inn
Aller Rd, Kingskerswell, Newton Abbot,
Devon TQ12 5AN
Tel: 01803 872130

Real Ales, Bar Food, Restaurant Menu,
Accommodation, No Smoking Area,
Disabled Facilities

7 The Bay Horse Inn
64 North St, Ashburton, Newton Abbot,
Devon TQ13 7QG
Tel: 01364 652838

Real Ales, Disabled Facilities

8 The Bay Horse Inn
8 Cistern St, Totnes, Devon TQ9 5SP
Tel: 01803 862088

Real Ales, Bar Food, Accommodation,
No Smoking Area

See panel on page 52

9 The Bay Hotel
15 Powderham Terrace, Teignmouth,
Devon TQ14 8BL
Tel: 01626 774123

Real Ales, Bar Food, Accommodation,
No Smoking Area, Disabled Facilities

10 The Bell Inn
108 Drew St, Brixham, Devon TQ5 9JY
Tel: 01803 851815

Real Ales, Bar Food

11 The Bickley Mill Inn
Stoneycombe, Newton Abbot,
Devon TQ12 5LN
Tel: 01803 873201

Real Ales, Bar Food, Restaurant Menu,
Accommodation, No Smoking Area

12 Birssyrs Bar
5 South Embankment, Dartmouth,
Devon TQ6 9BH
Tel: 01803 832998

Real Ales

13 Bishop John De Grandisson Inn
Clanage St, Bishopsteignton, Teignmouth,
Devon TQ14 9QS
Tel: 01626 775285

Real Ales, Bar Food

14 The Blagdon Inn
Totnes Rd, Paignton, Devon TQ4 7PU
Tel: 01803 521412

Real Ales, Bar Food, Restaurant Menu,
No Smoking Area

8 The Bay Horse Inn

8 Cistern Street, Totnes, Devon TQ9 5SP

☎ 01803 862088 Fax: 01803 840858

Real Ales, Bar Food, Accommodation, No Smoking Area

- ☛ 1 min walk from the centre of Totnes, yards from the A381
- 🍺 Doom Bar, Bass, Courage Best
- 🍴 12-3 & 7-9 (except Tuesday)
- 🛏 3 rooms (2 en suite)
- ⛱ Beer garden, pay & display opposite
- 💳 Major cards except Amex and Diners
- 🕐 11-3 & 6-11 Mon-Fri, 11-11 Sat, 11-3 & 6-10.30 Sun in Winter. Summer all day from 11am Mon -Sat & Noon Sun.
- 🏛 Bowden House 1 mile, Dartington Hall 2 miles, Paignton 4 miles, Torquay 6 miles

Totnes has claims to being the second oldest borough in the country, and no less an authority than Pevsner described it as 'one

of the most rewarding small towns in England'. Visitors to the **Bay Horse Inn** are rewarded with excellent hospitality from Jennifer and Ken, who are faring well in what is their first time running a pub together.

On a sloping street near the centre of town, just yards from the A381, the inn has an attractive exterior, whitewashed on the ground floor, slate-grey above, with window boxes making a colourful show in spring and summer. The oldest part of the premises date back as far as the 15th century, and there's a lovely traditional feel throughout, combined with the

comfort of armchairs and sofas and a bright, cheerful ambience generated by Jennifer, Ken and their friendly staff. At the back is a patio and a delightful lawned garden sheltered by trees and supplied with plenty of picnic benches. Bass, Sharps Doom Bar and Courage Best provide a choice for real ale connoisseurs. The Bay Horse is a very popular choice for diners, and the printed menu and daily changing specials board make the best use of fresh seasonal produce, much of it locally sourced. Seafood specials, steaks and the traditional roasts that are added to the Sunday choice are particular favourites, and booking is definitely recommended for Sunday lunch. The former pool room is being refurbished to provide extra bedrooms with disabled facilities

The Castle, the medieval town walls, the museums, the Guildhall and the Town Mill are among the many reasons for tarrying in Totnes, and the three guest bedrooms at the Bay Horse provide an ideal, well-located base for exploring this fascinating place.

15 The Blue Anchor

Teign St, Teignmouth, Devon TQ14 8EG
Tel: 01626 772741

Real Ales, Disabled Facilities

16 The Blue Anchor

83 Fore St, Brixham, Devon TQ5 8AH
Tel: 01803 859373

Real Ales, Bar Food, Restaurant Menu

17 The Brass Monkey

Hollands Rd, Teignmouth, Devon TQ14 8SR
Tel: 01626 773961

Real Ales

18 The Bridge Inn

Harford Rd, Ivybridge, Devon PL21 0AS
Tel: 01752 897086

Real Ales

19 Browns Hotel

27-29 Victoria Rd, Dartmouth, Devon TQ6 9RT
Tel: 01803 832572

Bar Food, Accommodation, No Smoking Area,
Disabled Facilities

20 Buckland Tout Saints Hotel

Buckland tout Saints, Kingsbridge,
Devon TQ7 2DS
Tel: 01548 853055

Bar Food, Restaurant Menu, Accommodation,
No Smoking Area

21 The Bull Inn

102 High St, Totnes, Devon TQ9 5SN
Tel: 01803 862042

Real Ales, Accommodation, Disabled Facilities

23 The Burton

Burton Street, Brixham, Devon PL8 2AH
☎ 01803 852805

Real Ales, Bar Food, Restaurant Menu

☛ 400 yards from the town centre, a short drive from the seafront

🍺 Courage Best, Bombardier

🍴 12-2.30 & 6-9 (Sun 12-4); no food Sun eve or Monday except Bank Holidays

⛱ Gardens, car park

🕐 Lunchtime and evening, all day Fri, Sat & Sun

🏛 Berry Head Country Park 1 mile, Torquay 5 miles

Situated a short walk from the town centre and harbour, the **Burton** has the friendliest of hosts in Andy and Lesley Walters. The inn offers warm and friendly atmosphere to visitors and regulars alike, and the bar, with a cosy open fire in cooler weather, is a great place to unwind with lively conversation and a glass of keg or cask ale. Andy is a top-notch chef, and dishes like his lasagne, curries, kebabs, and steak & ale deserve their strong following. Pizzas are another excellent choice, and the outstanding children's menu includes smaller portions of the 'grown-up' dishes. At the back of the pub is a delightful garden with plenty of chairs and picnic benches for enjoying an alfresco drink, a snack, a meal or the popular summer Sunday barbecue.

22 Bullers Arms

4 The Strand, Brixham, Devon TQ5 8EH
Tel: 01803 853329

Real Ales, Bar Food, Restaurant Menu,
No Smoking Area, Disabled Facilities

23 **Burton Hotel**

Burton St, Brixham, Devon TQ5 9HZ
Tel: 01803 852805

Real Ales, Bar Food, Restaurant Menu

See panel on page 53

24 The Butchers Arms

Abbotskerswell, Newton Abbot, Devon TQ12 5PE
Tel: 01626 360731

Real Ales, Bar Food, Restaurant Menu,
Disabled Facilities

25 The California Country Inn

California Cross, Modbury, Ivybridge,
Devon PL21 0SG
Tel: 01548 821449

Real Ales, Bar Food, Restaurant Menu,
No Smoking Area, Disabled Facilities

26 Castle Inn

Castle St, Totnes, Devon TQ9 5NU
Tel: 01803 863274

Real Ales, Bar Food

27 The Castle Inn

The Barnhay, Stoke Gabriel, Totnes,
Devon TQ9 6SA
Tel: 01803 782255

Real Ales, Bar Food, Restaurant Menu,
No Smoking Area

28 The Cherub Inn

11 Higher St, Dartmouth, Devon TQ6 9RB
Tel: 01803 832571

Real Ales, Bar Food, Restaurant Menu,
No Smoking Area

29 Church House Inn

Holne, Newton Abbot, Devon TQ13 7SJ
Tel: 01364 631208

Real Ales, Bar Food, Restaurant Menu,
Accommodation, No Smoking Area

30 Church House Inn

Stokenham, Kingsbridge, Devon TQ7 2SZ
Tel: 01548 580253

Real Ales, Bar Food, Restaurant Menu,
No Smoking Area

31 Church House Inn

Churchstow, Kingsbridge, Devon TQ7 3QW
Tel: 01548 852237

Real Ales, Bar Food, Restaurant Menu,
No Smoking Area, Disabled Facilities

32 Church House Inn

Harberton, Totnes, Devon TQ9 7SF
Tel: 01803 863707

Real Ales, Bar Food, Restaurant Menu,
Accommodation, No Smoking Area

33 The Church House Inn

Rattery, South Brent, Devon TQ10 9LD
Tel: 01364 642220

Real Ales, Bar Food, Restaurant Menu,
No Smoking Area, Disabled Facilities

34 The Church House Inn

Stokeinteignhead, Newton Abbot,
Devon TQ12 4QA
Tel: 01626 872475

Real Ales, Bar Food, Restaurant Menu,
No Smoking Area, Disabled Facilities

35 The Church House Inn

Church Walk, Stoke Gabriel, Totnes,
Devon TQ9 6SD
Tel: 01803 782384

Real Ales, Bar Food, No Smoking Area

36 Churston Court Inn

Church Rd, Churston Ferrers, Brixham,
Devon TQ5 0JE
Tel: 01803 842186

Real Ales, Bar Food, Restaurant Menu,
Accommodation, No Smoking Area,
Disabled Facilities

37 The Clifford Arms

34 Fore St, Shaldon, Teignmouth, Devon TQ14 0DE
Tel: 01626 872311

Real Ales, Bar Food, Restaurant Menu,
No Smoking Area, Disabled Facilities

See panel below

38 Cockhaven Manor

Cockhaven Rd Bishopsteignton, Teignmouth,
Devon TQ14 9RF
Tel: 01626 775252

Real Ales, Bar Food, Restaurant Menu,
Accommodation, No Smoking Area,
Disabled Facilities

See panel on page 56

39 Cottage Hotel Ltd

Hope, Kingsbridge, Devon TQ7 3HJ
Tel: 01548 561555

Bar Food, Restaurant Menu, Accommodation,
No Smoking Area, Disabled Facilities

40 Court Farm Inn

Abbotskerswell, Newton Abbot, Devon TQ12 5NY
Tel: 01626 361866

Real Ales, Bar Food, Restaurant Menu,
No Smoking Area

41 The Courtenay

45 Queen St, Newton Abbot, Devon TQ12 2AQ
Tel: 01626 351695

Real Ales, Bar Food, Disabled Facilities

42 Crabshell Inn

Crabshell/The Quay, Embankment Rd, Kingsbridge,
Devon TQ7 1JZ
Tel: 01548 852345

Real Ales, Bar Food, Restaurant Menu,
No Smoking Area

---

37 The Clifford Arms

Fore Street, Shaldon, Devon TQ14 0DE
☎ 01626 872311

**Real Ales, Bar Food, Restaurant Menu,
No Smoking Area, Disabled Facilities**

- On the A379 1 mile S of Teignmouth
- Reel Ale, Teignworthy
- 12-2 & 6-9 (no food Monday)
- Music Thursday eves in summer
- Patio
- Major cards accepted
- 11-3 & 5-11 (Sat & Sun all day)
- Teignmouth 1 mile, Torquay 8 miles

In the centre of Shaldon, on the opposite side of the Teign estuary from Teignmouth and linked to it by the A379, the **Clifford Arms** offers the best in hospitality, food and drink. Flowers and shrubs make a colourful show at the front of this fine old pub, and on a delightful little sheltered, paved terrace at the back. Bruce and Sam Theobald came here in the spring of 2004, and Bruce's talents in the kitchen are winning the pub a growing band of appreciative regulars. Some of his dishes are pub classics, while others are less familiar but equally well worth trying: how about trout and horseradish rillettes with a pickled cucumber relish, or sweet potato gnocchi with an artichoke and mushroom sauce? The bar keeps plenty of West Country ales to accompany a meal or enjoy on their own.

38 Cockhaven Manor Inn

Cockhaven Road, Bishopsteignton,
Devon TQ14 9RF

☎ 01626 775252 🌐 www.cockhavenmanor.com

**Real Ales, Bar Food, Restaurant Menu,
Accommodation, No Smoking Area,
Disabled Facilities**

 In a residential part of Bishopsteignton off the A381 between Newton Abbot and Teignmouth.

 Selection

 12-2 & 6.30-9.30

 12 rooms

 Garden, car park

 Major cards accepted

🕐 11-2.30 & 6-11, 7 days a week

🏛 Church and Museum in Bishopsteignton; Teignmouth 2 miles, Newton Abbot 3 miles, Dawlish 4 miles

Bishopsteignton is a substantial village off the Teign estuary, with a church containing some of the finest Norman craftsmanship in the county and a fascinating museum of local

life. Another excellent reason for visiting Bishopsteignton is the **Cockhaven Manor Inn**, a handsome building in a quiet setting behind trim lawns and bushes just off the A381.

This splendid inn, whose oldest parts date back to the 16th century, has attracted a large and loyal local following ever since it was acquired by Roy and Amanda Extance, and the word is getting out that this is a place definitely worth a detour. A fine selection of drinks is served in the comfortable bar, and in the elegant, softly-lit restaurant lunchers and diners are treated to a feast of the very best of West Country food.

The regular menu and daily specials tempt with a mouthwatering choice that caters for both traditional and more adventurous tastes: typical dishes could include wild boar & apple sausages, grilled salmon steak with tomato garlic sauce, duck breast with a plum glaze, fillet of beef teriyaki and, for vegetarians, goat's cheese, plum tomato and red onion tartlet. Desserts keep the enjoyment levels high to the end, and the fine food is accompanied by a well-chosen selection of wines.

Cockhaven Manor is not a place for dashing in and out, and its 12 beautifully appointed en suite bedrooms provide an ideal choice for a relaxing break or a touring holiday. Top of the range are the romantic four-poster rooms, but all the rooms offer very high standards of décor and comfort. The Manor is also a favourite venue for meetings, functions, parties, wedding receptions and other special occasions.

44   The Cricket Inn

Beesands, nr Kingsbridge, Devon TQ7 2EN

☎ 01548 580215

Real Ales, Bar Food, Restaurant Menu, Accommodation, No Smoking Area, Disabled Facilities

- ☞ Take the A379 towards Dartmouth and turn right at Chillington for Beesands
- 🍺 Bass, London Pride
- 🍴 12-2.30 & 6-9 (not Sun eve in winter)
- 🛏 En suite rooms
- ⚓ Garden, car park
- 💳 Major cards accepted
- 🕐 L & D (all day in summer)
- 🏛 Kingsbridge 5 miles, Dartmouth 8 miles

The Cricket Inn is a distinguished old pub that Rachel Simon and Nigel Heath rescued from disrepair when they took it over in 2001. The interior is decorated with old maps, charts and local photographs, and the horseshoe-shaped bar, a centre of village life, is stocked with a full selection of local ales and other beers, lagers, ciders, wines and spirits. Literally just across the road from the sea, the Cricket is known far outside the area for its home cooking, particularly the seafood dishes. Most of the fish is landed locally, some of it by Nigel himself at Chillington. The crab sandwiches and salads and the scallops are justly renowned, while meat-eaters can tuck into succulent steaks and the traditional Sunday roasts. Beesands is known for its mile-long shingle beach, and guests staying overnight at the Cricket can look forward to a super breakfast that will set them up for walks in the bracing sea air.

---

43   Creeks End Inn

Squares Quay, Kingsbridge, Devon TQ7 1HZ
Tel: 01548 853434

Real Ales, Bar Food

44   The Cricket Inn

Beesands, Kingsbridge, Devon TQ7 2EN
Tel: 01548 580215

Real Ales, Bar Food, Restaurant Menu, Accommodation, No Smoking Area, Disabled Facilities

See panel above

45   The Dart Marina Hotel

Sandquay Rd, Dartmouth, Devon TQ6 9QR
Tel: 01803 832580

Real Ales, Bar Food, Restaurant Menu, Accommodation, No Smoking Area, Disabled Facilities

46   Dartbridge Inn

Totnes Rd, Buckfastleigh, Devon TQ11 0JR
Tel: 01364 642214

Real Ales, Bar Food, Restaurant Menu, Accommodation, No Smoking Area, Disabled Facilities

47   The Dartmoor Halfway Inn

Travellers Rest, Bickington, Newton Abbot, Devon TQ12 6JW
Tel: 01626 821270

Real Ales, Bar Food, Restaurant Menu, Accommodation, No Smoking Area

48   Dartmoor Lodge Hotel

Ashburton, Newton Abbot, Devon TQ13 7JW
Tel: 01364 652232

Real Ales, Bar Food, Restaurant Menu, Accommodation, No Smoking Area, Disabled Facilities

49 Dartmouth Arms

26 Lower St, Dartmouth, Devon TQ6 9AN
Tel: 01803 832903

Real Ales, Bar Food

50 Dartmouth Golf and Country Club

Blackawton, Totnes, Devon TQ9 7DE
Tel: 01803 712686

Real Ales, Bar Food, Restaurant Menu,
Accommodation, No Smoking Area

51 The Dartmouth Inn

63 East St, Newton Abbot, Devon TQ12 2JP
Tel: 01626 353451

Real Ales, Disabled Facilities

52 The Dartmouth Inn

28 Warland, Totnes, Devon TQ9 5EL
Tel: 01803 863252

Real Ales, Bar Food, Restaurant Menu,
No Smoking Area

53 Deer Park Inn

Dartmouth Rd, Stoke Fleming, Dartmouth,
Devon TQ6 0RF
Tel: 01803 770755

Real Ales, Bar Food, Restaurant Menu,
Accommodation, No Smoking Area,
Disabled Facilities

54 Devon Arms Hotel

Northumberland Place, Teignmouth,
Devon TQ14 8DE
Tel: 01626 774400

Real Ales, Bar Food, Restaurant Menu,
Accommodation

55 The Devon Dumpling

108 Shiphay Lane, Torquay, Devon TQ2 7BY
Tel: 01803 613465

Real Ales, Bar Food

56 The Dew Drop Inn

66 Fore St, Kingsteignton, Newton Abbot,
Devon TQ12 3AU
Tel: 01626 352786

Real Ales

57 Dicey O'Reilly

Regent St, Teignmouth, Devon TQ14 8SX
Tel: 01626 779055

Bar Food, Disabled Facilities

58 Dodbrooke Inn

Church St, Kingsbridge, Devon TQ7 1DB
Tel: 01548 852068

Real Ales, Bar Food, Restaurant Menu,
No Smoking Area

59 The Dolphin

5 Market St, Dartmouth, Devon TQ6 9QE
Tel: 01803 833835

Real Ales, Restaurant Menu, No Smoking Area,
Disabled Facilities

60 The Dolphin Inn

Dolphin, Kingston, Kingsbridge, Devon TQ7 4QE
Tel: 01548 810314

Real Ales, Bar Food, Accommodation,
No Smoking Area, Disabled Facilities

61 Drakes Hotel

33 Northumberland Place, Teignmouth,
Devon TQ14 8BU
Tel: 01626 772777

Bar Food, Restaurant Menu, Accommodation,
Disabled Facilities

62 Duke Of Cornwall Inn

3 Keaton Rd, Ivybridge, Devon PL21 9DH
Tel: 01752 892867

Real Ales, Bar Food, Restaurant Menu,
No Smoking Area

63 The Durant Arms

Ashprington, Totnes, Devon TQ9 7UP
Tel: 01803 732240

Real Ales, Bar Food, Restaurant Menu,
Accommodation, No Smoking Area

64 The Endeavour
31 Northumberland Place, Teignmouth,
Devon TQ14 8BU
Tel: 01626 773534

Disabled Facilities

65 English House Restaurant
Teignmouth Rd, Maidencombe, Torquay,
Devon TQ1 4SY
Tel: 01803 328760

Restaurant Menu, Accommodation,
No Smoking Area

66 The Exchange
Fore St, Ivybridge, Devon PL21 9AB
Tel: 01752 896677

Real Ales, Bar Food, No Smoking Area

---

67 The Exeter Inn
Church Street, Modbury, Devon PL21 0QR
☎ 01548 830239   ⊕ www.exeter-inn.ltd.uk

**Real Ales, Bar Food, Restaurant Menu,
No Smoking Area**

- ☛ Centrally located in Modbury (A379)
- 🍺 Doom Bar, Greene King IPA
- 🍴 12-2.30 & 6-9 (not Sun eve)
- 🛏 6 en suite rooms
- 🎵 Quiz Wednesday
- ⚓ Beer garden
- 💳 Major cards except Amex
- 🕐 L & D (all day in summer)
- 🏛 Ivybridge 4 miles, Kingsbridge 7 miles

The **Exeter Inn** is a pub of great charm and character. The rambling public area has an old-world look bestowed by flagstones, beams and period pictures and prints, and at the back is a delightful tucked-away garden. Hosts Lillian and John and their chef offer an excellent selection of good wholesome dishes, with a choice of at least three real ales to accompany. The Exeter has six en suite rooms for B&B

67 Exeter Inn
Church St, Modbury, Ivybridge,
Devon PL21 0QR
Tel: 01548 830239

Real Ales, Bar Food, Restaurant Menu,
No Smoking Area

See panel adjacent

68 Exeter Inn
26 West St, Ashburton, Newton Abbot,
Devon TQ13 7DU
Tel: 01364 652013

Real Ales, Bar Food

69 F & R's Bar
19 Northumberland Place, Teignmouth,
Devon TQ14 8BZ
Tel: 01626 879186

Real Ales, Bar Food, Restaurant Menu

70 Ferry Boat Inn
Manor St, Dittisham, Dartmouth,
Devon TQ6 0EX
Tel: 01803 722368

Real Ales, Bar Food, Restaurant Menu,
No Smoking Area

71 The Ferry Boat Inn
The Strand Shaldon, Teignmouth,
Devon TQ14 0DL
Tel: 01626 872340

Real Ales, Bar Food, Restaurant Menu,
No Smoking Area, Disabled Facilities

72 The Ferry Inn
Fore St, Salcombe, Devon TQ8 8JE
Tel: 01548 844000

Real Ales, Bar Food, Restaurant Menu,
No Smoking Area

73 Floating Bridge Inn
Coombe Rd, Dartmouth, Devon TQ6 9PQ
Tel: 01803 832354

Real Ales, Bar Food, Restaurant Menu,
No Smoking Area, Disabled Facilities

75 The Forest Inn

Hexworthy, Dartmoor, Devon PL20 6SD

☎ 01364 631211 ⊕ www.theforestinn.co.uk

Real Ales, Bar Food, Restaurant Menu,
Accommodation, No Smoking Area,
Disabled Facilities

- ☛ Signposted off the B3357 north of Buckfastleigh
- 🍺 Teignworthy and others
- 🍴 12-2 & 7-9 (all day in summer)
- 🛏 10 rooms en suite or private bathrooms
- ⛲ Garden, car park
- 💳 Major cards except Diners
- 🕐 12-11
- 🏛 Princetown 4 miles, Buckfastleigh 8 miles

The accommodation offers a choice between 10 well-equipped guest rooms in the main building (seven en suite, the rest with dedicated private facilities) and a 20-bedded budget bunkhouse with showers and a kitchenette. Guests in the main part of the inn are welcome to bring their dogs, and stabling can be arranged for horses. Duchy of

The **Forest Inn** provides the perfect base for exploring Dartmoor. It lies hidden away in the lanes north of Buckfastleigh, signposted from the B3357 Dartmeet to Two Bridges road, but despite the remote setting it has become a popular spot with visitors to the area as well as local people.

This popularity is due in no small measure to hosts James and Irene Glenister, who provide their customers with outstanding hospitality and a warm, relaxing ambience for a drink, a snack, a meal or a short break or longer stay. The stunning natural beauty of Dartmoor is on the doorstep, and walkers, anglers, cyclists, canoeists and motorists are all equally welcome.

Cornwall fishing permits are available for holders of a current NRA licence.

Two or three real ales from the local Teignworthy Brewery and local ciders quench fresh-air thirsts, and the bar features handsome panelling below and above the service counter and brass foot and hand rails. In the lounge area, where a log fire blazes away on chilly days, visitors can relax on comfortable sofas.

An extensive choice of light snacks is available in the Huccaby Room, while in the restaurant delicious home-cooked dishes are based on the best local produce. After an invigorating few hours exploring the area, dishes like braised lamb shanks and boozy beef pie really hit the mark, but the menus offer something for all tastes and appetites.

74 The Forces Tavern

The Forces Tavern, Blackawton, Totnes,
Devon TQ9 7DJ
Tel: 01803 712226

Real Ales, Bar Food, Restaurant Menu,
Accommodation, No Smoking Area,
Disabled Facilities

75 The Forest Inn

Hexworthy, Dartmoor, Devon PL20 6SD
Tel: 01364 631211

Real Ales, Bar Food, Restaurant Menu,
Accommodation, No Smoking Area,
Disabled Facilities

See panel opposite

76 Fortescue Arms

East Allington, Totnes, Devon TQ9 7RA
Tel: 01548 521215

Real Ales, Bar Food, Restaurant Menu,
Accommodation, No Smoking Area

77 Fortescue Inn

Union St, Salcombe, Devon TQ8 8BZ
Tel: 01548 842868

Real Ales, Bar Food, Restaurant Menu,
No Smoking Area, Disabled Facilities

See panel below

78 The Fox

13 Queen St, Newton Abbot, Devon TQ12 2AQ
Tel: 01626 354238

Real Ales, Bar Food, Disabled Facilities

See panel on page 62

79 George & Dragon

Mayors Avenue, Dartmouth, Devon TQ6 9NG
Tel: 01803 832325

Real Ales, Bar Food, Restaurant Menu,
Accommodation

---

77 The Fortescue Inn

Union Street, Salcombe, Devon TQ8 8BZ
☎ 01548 842868

**Real Ales, Bar Food, Restaurant Menu,
No Smoking Area, Disabled Facilities**

☛ Centrally located in Salcombe
🍺 Otter, Bass, Courage Directors
🍴 12-4 (winter to 2.30) & 7-9.30
💳 Major cards except Amex or Diners
🕐 11-11
🏛 Overbecks NT 2 miles, Kingsbridge 4 miles

In the very heart of Salcombe town you will find **The Fortescue Inn,** a lovely old whitewashed stone building. Having beautiful surroundings and only 50 yards from the sea it makes the ideal place to enjoy a drink or a meal from the extensive menu, or specials board that changes daily. A good wine list and a large selection of well kept ales are available. A lot of the fish and meat is local and all the food is freshly prepared by the Chef and his team.

There's no wonder this is a favourite spot for both locals and tourists, so it is advisable to book during the busy season. If you prefer a more lively night out, The Ships bar is the place to go. With juke box, pool table, big screen TV and regular live music you will find it hard not to have a good time. In summer nightly BBQ's are held in the beer garden. What ever you choose to do at the Fortescue, Val, Mike and their friendly staff will make sure you enjoy yourself.

78 The Fox

13 Queen Street, Newton Abbot, Devon TQ12 2AQ
☎ 01626 354238

Real Ales, Bar Food, Disabled Facilities

☛ On a prime site in the centre of Newton Abbot

🍺 Bass

🍴 12-3

🎵 Live music Sun eve

🕐 11-11

🏛 Newton Abbot racecourse 1 mile

On one of the main streets in the ancient market town of Newton Abbot, the **Fox** is one of the best-known pubs in the region, and its regular customers are drawn from all ages. Behind the elegant Georgian frontage – painted blue at street level, whitewashed above, with gold signage and colourful hanging baskets and window boxes – the interior is light and airy, with pristine white walls, wooden floors and some handsome panelling. The long bar is divided into several sections, some with cosy booth seating, and at one end is a big TV screen for major sports events. Landlord Wayne Leaver, assisted by cheerful, on-the-ball staff, has made many new friends since arriving in 2003, making this a popular sport for enjoying a glass or two of real ale, Worthington Creamflow, Carling or Stella. Snacks, jacket potatoes and steaks are among the food options served every lunchtime.

80 George Inn
Main St, Blackawton, Totnes, Devon TQ9 7BG
Tel: 01803 712342

Real Ales, Bar Food, Restaurant Menu, Accommodation, No Smoking Area

81 The Globe
61 Fore St, Brixham, Devon TQ5 8AG
Tel: 01803 882154

Real Ales, Bar Food, Restaurant Menu, No Smoking Area

82 The Globe Inn
123 Plymouth Rd, Buckfastleigh, Devon TQ11 0DA
Tel: 01364 642223

Real Ales, Bar Food, Restaurant Menu, Accommodation, No Smoking Area, Disabled Facilities

See panel opposite

83 The Globe Inn
Frogmore, Kingsbridge, Devon TQ7 2NR
Tel: 01548 531351

Real Ales, Bar Food, Restaurant Menu, Accommodation, No Smoking Area

84 The Golden Lion
Market St, Newton Abbot, Devon TQ12 2RB
Tel: 01626 367062

Real Ales

85 The Green Dragon
Church St, Stoke Fleming, Dartmouth, Devon TQ6 0PX
Tel: 01803 770238

Real Ales, Bar Food, Restaurant Menu, No Smoking Area

86 The Green Man
67 East St, Newton Abbot, Devon TQ12 2JR
Tel: 01626 337653

No Smoking Area

87 The Hare & Hounds

Torquay Rd, Kingskerswell, Newton Abbot,
Devon TQ12 5HH
Tel: 01803 873119

Real Ales, Bar Food, Restaurant Menu,
No Smoking Area, Disabled Facilities

88 The Heavitree Arms

24-26 Highweek Rd, Newton Abbot,
Devon TQ12 1TP
Tel: 01626 353116

Bar Food, No Smoking Area, Disabled Facilities

89 The Hermitage Inn

8 Mill St, Kingsbridge, Devon TQ7 1ED
Tel: 01548 853234

Real Ales, Bar Food

90 The Highweek Village Inn

10 Highweek Village, Newton Abbot,
Devon TQ12 1QA
Tel: 01626 356490

Real Ales, Bar Food, Restaurant Menu,
No Smoking Area

91 Hope & Anchor Inn

Hope Cove, Kingsbridge, Devon TQ7 3HQ
Tel: 01548 561294

Real Ales, Bar Food, Restaurant Menu,
Accommodation, No Smoking Area,
Disabled Facilities

92 Horse & Groom

Bittaford, Ivybridge, Devon PL21 0EL
Tel: 01752 892358

Real Ales, Bar Food, Restaurant Menu

93 The Hunters Lodge Inn

Cornworthy, Totnes, Devon TQ9 7ES
Tel: 01803 732204

Real Ales, Bar Food, Restaurant Menu,
No Smoking Area

94 The Imperial

28 Western Rd, Ivybridge, Devon PL21 9AN
Tel: 01752 892269

Real Ales, Bar Food, Restaurant Menu,
No Smoking Area, Disabled Facilities

82 The Globe Inn

123 Plymouth Road, Buckfastleigh,
Devon TQ11 0DA

☎ 01364 642233   🌐 www.theglobeinn.biz

**Real Ales, Bar Food, Restaurant Menu,
Accommodation, No Smoking Area,
Disabled Facilities**

☞ In the heart of Buckfastleigh, on the B3380 2 miles SW of Ashburton

🍺 Otter, Courage Directors

🍴 12-2 & 7-9

🛏 5 en suite rooms

🎵 Quiz Monday

⚓ Beer garden

💳 Major cards accepted

🕐 Lunchtime and evening

🏛 Many places of interest in Buckfastleigh

Close to both Dartmoor and the South Hams, Buckfastleigh and the surrounding area have plenty for the visitor to see and do, and the **Globe Inn** provides an ideal base for touring the region. This former coaching inn on a prominent corner site retains many period features, and the bar and dining area are roomy, warm and comfortable. Blue-painted wooden panelling is an eyecatching feature on the walls and the front of the bar counter. Alan and Jacqui Butler always keep three real ales on tap, and in the non-smoking restaurant lunchtimes and evenings bring a good selection of wholesome home-cooked dishes. Booking is advisable to be sure of a table on Friday and Saturday evenings and Sunday lunchtime. The five en suite bedrooms, all upstairs, include one room big enough for a family.

95 The John Bull

68 70 Chatto Rd, Torquay, Devon TQ1 4UH
Tel: 01803 328288

Real Ales, Bar Food, Accommodation,
No Smoking Area

96 The Jolly Abbot

16 East St, Newton Abbot, Devon TQ12 1AG
Tel: 01626 365378

Real Ales, Bar Food

97 The Jolly Farmer

8 Market St, Newton Abbot, Devon TQ12 2RB
Tel: 01626 354010

Real Ales, Bar Food, Restaurant Menu,
No Smoking Area, Disabled Facilities

98 The Jolly Sailor

Ogwell, Newton Abbot, Devon TQ12 6AW
Tel: 01626 354581

Real Ales, Bar Food, Restaurant Menu,
No Smoking Area, Disabled Facilities

99 The Journeys End Inn

Ringmore, Kingsbridge, Devon TQ7 4HL
Tel: 01548 810205

Real Ales, Bar Food, Restaurant Menu,
No Smoking Area

100 Keyberry Hotel

17 Kingskerswell Rd, Newton Abbot,
Devon TQ12 1DQ
Tel: 01626 352120

Real Ales, Bar Food, Restaurant Menu,
Accommodation, No Smoking Area,
Disabled Facilities

101 The King of Prussia

Church St, Kingsbridge, Devon TQ7 1JB
Tel: 01548 852099

Real Ales, Bar Food

102 The Kings Arms

14-15 Fore St, Buckfastleigh, Devon TQ11 0BT
Tel: 01364 642341

Real Ales, Bar Food, Restaurant Menu,
Accommodation, Disabled Facilities

103 The Kings Arms

6 Oakford, Kingsteignton, Newton Abbot,
Devon TQ12 3EG
Tel: 01626 364859

Real Ales, Bar Food, Disabled Facilities

104 The Kings Arms

Regent Gardens, Teignmouth, Devon TQ14 8SU
Tel: 01626 775268

Real Ales, Bar Food, Accommodation

105 The Kings Arms

20 Fore St, Salcombe, Devon TQ8 8BU
Tel: 01548 842202

Real Ales, Bar Food, Restaurant Menu,
No Smoking Area

106 The Kings Arms Hotel

93 Fore St, Kingsbridge, Devon TQ7 1AB
Tel: 01548 852071

Real Ales, Bar Food, Restaurant Menu,
Accommodation, No Smoking Area,
Disabled Facilities

107 Kings Arms Inn

Strete, Dartmouth, Devon TQ6 0RW
Tel: 01803 770377

Real Ales, Bar Food, Restaurant Menu,
No Smoking Area, Disabled Facilities

108 The Kingsbridge Inn

9 Leechwell St, Totnes, Devon TQ9 5SY
Tel: 01803 863324

Real Ales, Bar Food, Restaurant Menu,
No Smoking Area

109 The Lifeboat Inn

6 Strand, Teignmouth, Devon TQ14 8BW
Tel: 01626 774354

Real Ales

110 The Linny Inn

Coffinswell, Newton Abbot, Devon TQ12 4SR
Tel: 01803 873192

Real Ales, Bar Food, Restaurant Menu,
No Smoking Area, Disabled Facilities

111 Live & Let Live Inn

Landscove, Ashburton, Newton Abbot,
Devon TQ13 7LZ
Tel: 01803 762663

Real Ales, Bar Food, No Smoking Area

112 Locomotive Inn

35-37 East St, Newton Abbot, Devon TQ12 2JP
Tel: 01626 365249

Real Ales, Disabled Facilities

113 Loddiswell Inn

Loddiswell, Kingsbridge, Devon TQ7 4QJ
Tel: 01548 550308

Real Ales, Bar Food, Restaurant Menu,
No Smoking Area, Disabled Facilities

See panel below

---

113 Loddiswell Inn

Loddiswell, nr Kingsbridge, Devon TQ7 4QJ

☎ 01548 550308   ⊕ www.loddiswellinn.co.uk

**Real Ales, Bar Food, Restaurant Menu,
No Smoking Area, Disabled Facilities**

- ☛ On the B3196 3 miles N of Kingsbridge
- 🍺 Three rotating
- 🍴 12-2 & 6-9
- 🛏 3 rooms (2 en suite)
- 🎵 Regular quiz and folk nights, summer disco and karaoke
- ⛲ Patio
- 💳 Major cards except Amex
- 🕐 Lunchtime and evening
- 🏛 St Andrews Wood 1 mile, Kingsbridge 3 miles, Salcombe 6 miles

A friendly greeting from Roger and Sally is assured at the **Loddiswell Inn**, set in the picturesque South Hams district. A good selection of real ales, lagers and wines is served in the bar, and an extensive variety of dishes is served every lunchtime and evening – steaks are a speciality. Three guest bedrooms have recently come on stream at this popular inn.

114 London Inn

The Green, Shaldon, Teignmouth,
Devon TQ14 0DN
Tel: 01626 872453

Real Ales, Bar Food, Restaurant Menu

115 London Inn Hotel

Exeter Rd, South Brent, Devon TQ10 9DF
Tel: 01364 73223

Real Ales, Bar Food, Restaurant Menu,
Accommodation, No Smoking Area

116 The Long Bar

Union Lane, Brixham, Devon TQ5 8DY
Tel: 01803 853110

Disabled Facilities

117 The Lord Nelson

Fore St, Kingskerswell, Newton Abbot,
Devon TQ12 5JB
Tel: 01803 873361

Real Ales

118 Lord Nelson Inn

7 Fore St, Totnes, Devon TQ9 5DA
Tel: 01803 866015

Real Ales, No Smoking Area

119 The Malsters Arms

Tuckenhay, Totnes, Devon TQ9 7EQ
Tel: 01803 732350

Real Ales, Bar Food, Restaurant Menu,
Accommodation, No Smoking Area

120 Manor Inn

2 Stoke Gabriel Rd, Galmpton, Brixham,
Devon TQ5 0NL
Tel: 01803 842346

Real Ales, Bar Food, Restaurant Menu,
No Smoking Area, Disabled Facilities

121 Manor Inn

28 Higher St, Brixham, Devon TQ5 8HW
Tel: 01803 882366

Real Ales, Bar Food

135 The Old Chapel Inn

St Ann's Chapel, nr Bigbury-on-Sea,
Devon TQ7 4HQ

☎ 01548 810241 🌐 www.oldchapelinn.com

**Real Ales, Bar Food, Restaurant Menu,
Accommodation, No Smoking Area,
Disabled Facilities**

☞ Take the B3392 Bigbury-on-Sea road at
Ashford or Modbury off the A379 Plymouth-
Kingsbridge road

🍶 Local ales

🍴 12-2.30 & 7-9.30 (bar meals earlier)

🛏 5 en suite rooms

🅿 Car park

💳 Major cards accepted

🕐 L & D (all day in summer)

🏛 Bigbury ½ mile, Bigbury-on-Sea 2½ miles,
Kingsbridge 8 miles

Owners Paul and Britt Clement have completely transformed the **Old Chapel Inn**, which stands on a corner site at St Ann's Chapel, half a mile from Bigbury and two miles from Bigbury-on-Sea. At the heart of the inn lies the ancient St Ann's Chapel with its unique vaulted hammerbeam roof and a holy well. In the equally atmospheric Refectory Restaurant head chef Darren Dickinson insists on the very best fresh, seasonal raw materials, including fish landed at Plymouth, Salcombe and Brixham and fully traceable meat. The five en suite rooms, with hand-made beds, sumptuous fabrics and original art on the walls, provide the perfect base for a break, relaxing in the inn's immaculate garden, strolling by the sea, lazing on the beach, walking in the lanes, fishing, riding or enjoying a round of golf.

136 The Old Church House Inn

Torbryan, Devon TQ12 5UR

☎ 01803 812372 www.oldchurchhouseinn.co.uk

**Real Ales, Bar Food, Restaurant Menu,
Accommodation, No Smoking Area**

☞ Follow signs to Denbury and Woodland off the
southbound carriageway of the A38 nr
Ashburton. After 2 miles, see signs for Torbryan

🍶 Selection

🍴 12-2.30 & 7-9.30

🛏 15 en suite rooms

🅿 Garden, car park

💳 Major cards accepted

🕐 All day

🏛 Dartington 5 miles, Ashburton 5 miles,
Newton Abbot 6 miles

Resident proprietors Kane and Carolynne Clarke provide excellent hospitality at the **Old Church House Inn**, a wonderfully atmospheric 13th century hostelry in a tranquil country setting. Comfort is a byword in the public rooms, where ancient beams and winter log fires add to the charm, and the sitting room beckons with its inviting sofas and armchairs. Locally brewed cask ales and ciders are always on tap, and the bar stocks an impressive range and a wide choice of fine whiskies and single malts. The chefs make splendid use of local produce on the extensive menu, and the food is complemented by a comprehensive wine list. The guest accommodation is also very comfortable and full of character, each of the en suite bedrooms having its own individual appeal, and the inn's owners and staff ensure that any stay, short or long, is memorable.

122 Maritime Inn
79 King St, Brixham, Devon TQ5 9TH
Tel: 01803 853535

Real Ales, Accommodation, Disabled Facilities

123 Market House Inn
3 Market St, Newton Abbot, Devon TQ12 2RJ
Tel: 01626 201013

Real Ales

124 Market House Inn
Market St, Dartmouth, Devon TQ6 9QE
Tel: 01803 832128

Real Ales, Bar Food, Restaurant Menu

125 Mill At Avonwick
South Brent, Devon TQ10 9ES
Tel: 01364 72488

Real Ales, Bar Food, Restaurant Menu,
No Smoking Area, Disabled Facilities

126 Millbrook Inn
South Pool, Kingsbridge, Devon TQ7 2RW
Tel: 01548 531581

Real Ales, Bar Food, Restaurant Menu,
No Smoking Area

127 The Modbury Inn
Brownston St, Modbury, Ivybridge,
Devon PL21 0RQ
Tel: 01548 830275

Real Ales, Bar Food, Restaurant Menu,
Accommodation, No Smoking Area

128 Molloys
1 Teign St, Teignmouth, Devon TQ14 8EA
Tel: 01626 774661

Real Ales, Bar Food, Restaurant Menu

129 Monks Retreat
The Monks Retreat, Broadhempston, Totnes,
Devon TQ9 6BN
Tel: 01803 812203

Real Ales, Bar Food, Restaurant Menu,
No Smoking Area

130 The Ness House Hotel
Ness Drive, Shaldon, Teignmouth,
Devon TQ14 0HP
Tel: 01626 873480

Bar Food, Restaurant Menu, Accommodation,
No Smoking Area, Disabled Facilities

131 The New Inn
Higher Town, Malborough, Devon TQ7 3RL
Tel: 01548 561320

Real Ales, Bar Food, Restaurant Menu,
No Smoking Area

132 The New Inn
Moreleigh, Totnes, Devon TQ9 7JH
Tel: 01548 821326

Real Ales, Bar Food, Restaurant Menu,
No Smoking Area, Disabled Facilities

133 The New Quay Inn
New Quay St, Teignmouth, Devon TQ14 8DA
Tel: 01626 774145

Real Ales, Bar Food, Accommodation

134 Noahs Ark
Totnes Rd, Paignton, Devon TQ4 7HB
Tel: 01803 558351

Real Ales, Bar Food, No Smoking Area,
Disabled Facilities

135 The Old Chapel Inn
St Ann's Chapel, Kingsbridge, Devon TQ7 4HQ
Tel: 01548 810241

Real Ales, Bar Food, Restaurant Menu,
Accommodation, No Smoking Area,
Disabled Facilities

See panel opposite

136 Old Church House Inn
Torbryan, Nr Newton Abbot, Devon TQ12 5UR
Tel: 01803 812372

Real Ales, Bar Food, Restaurant Menu,
Accommodation, No Smoking Area

See panel opposite

137 Old Inn

Halwell, Totnes, Devon TQ9 7JA
Tel: 01803 712329

Real Ales, Bar Food, Restaurant Menu,
Accommodation, No Smoking Area,
Disabled Facilities

138 The Old Smithy

45 Fore St, Ivybridge, Devon PL21 9AE
Tel: 01752 892490

Real Ales, Disabled Facilities

139 The Open Arms

Chillington, Kingsbridge, Devon TQ7 2LD
Tel: 01548 581171

Real Ales, Bar Food, Restaurant Menu,
No Smoking Area, Disabled Facilities

140 Orestone Manor Hotel

Rockhouse Lane, Maidencombe, Torquay,
Devon TQ1 4SX
Tel: 01803 328098

Restaurant Menu, Accommodation

141 The Pack Horse

Plymouth Rd, South Brent, Devon TQ10 9BH
Tel: 01364 72283

Bar Food, Restaurant Menu, Accommodation,
No Smoking Area

142 The Park Inn

15 Coles Lane, Newton Abbot,
Devon TQ12 5BQ
Tel: 01803 872216

Real Ales, No Smoking Area

143 Parkers Arms

343-347 Totnes Rd, Paignton, Devon TQ4 7DE
Tel: 01803 551011

Real Ales, Bar Food, Restaurant Menu,
No Smoking Area, Disabled Facilities

144 The Passage House Inn

Hackney Lane, Kingsteignton, Newton Abbot,
Devon TQ12 3QH
Tel: 01626 353243

Real Ales, Bar Food, Accommodation,
No Smoking Area, Disabled Facilities

145 Pen Inn

Torquay Rd, Newton Abbot, Devon TQ12 4AQ
Tel: 01626 354661

Real Ales, Bar Food, Restaurant Menu,
No Smoking Area

146 The Pig & Whistle

Newton Rd, Littlehempston, Totnes,
Devon TQ9 6LT
Tel: 01803 863733

Real Ales, Bar Food, Restaurant Menu,
No Smoking Area

147 Pigs Nose Inn

East Prawle, Kingsbridge, Devon TQ7 2BY
Tel: 01548 511209

Real Ales, Bar Food, Restaurant Menu,
No Smoking Area, Disabled Facilities

148 The Plough Inn

Haytor Drive, Newton Abbot,
Devon TQ12 4DU
Tel: 01626 365597

Real Ales, Bar Food, Restaurant Menu,
Accommodation, No Smoking Area,
Disabled Facilities

149 The Plough Inn

Fore St, Ipplepen, Newton Abbot,
Devon TQ12 5RP
Tel: 01803 812118

Real Ales, Bar Food, Restaurant Menu,
No Smoking Area, Disabled Facilities

150 Port Light Hotel

Bolberry, Malborough, Kingsbridge,
Devon TQ7 3DY
Tel: 01548 561384

Real Ales, Bar Food, Restaurant Menu,
Accommodation, No Smoking Area

151 The Providence

East Prawle, Kingsbridge, Devon TQ7 2BU
Tel: 01548 511208

Real Ales, Bar Food, Accommodation,
No Smoking Area

152 The Quay
1-3 Fore St, Kingsbridge, Devon TQ7 1PG
Tel: 01548 852231

Real Ales

153 Quayside Hotel
41-49 King St, Brixham, Devon TQ5 9TJ
Tel: 01803 855751

Bar Food, Restaurant Menu, No Smoking Area,
Disabled Facilities

154 Queens Arms
31 Station Hill, Brixham, Devon TQ5 9JU
Tel: 01803 852074

Real Ales

155 The Queens Arms
Slapton, Kingsbridge, Devon TQ7 2PN
Tel: 01548 580800

Real Ales, Bar Food

156 Queens Hotel
Queen St, Newton Abbot, Devon TQ12 2EZ
Tel: 01626 363133

Real Ales, Bar Food, Accommodation,
No Smoking Area

157 Railway Hotel
197 Queen St, Newton Abbot,
Devon TQ12 2BS
Tel: 01626 354166

Real Ales, Bar Food, Disabled Facilities

158 The Red Lion Inn
The Level, Dittisham, Dartmouth,
Devon TQ6 0ES
Tel: 01803 722235

Real Ales, Bar Food, Restaurant Menu,
Accommodation, No Smoking Area

159 Ring O'Bells
Fore St, Teignmouth, Devon TQ14 9QP
Tel: 01626 775468

Real Ales, Bar Food, Restaurant Menu,
No Smoking Area, Disabled Facilities

160 Ring O'Bells
West Alvington, Kingsbridge, Devon TQ7 3PG
Tel: 01548 852437

Real Ales, Bar Food, Restaurant Menu,
Accommodation, No Smoking Area,
Disabled Facilities

161 The Rising Sun
The Quay, Brixham, Devon TQ5 8AW
Tel: 01803 853236

Real Ales, Bar Food, Restaurant Menu,
No Smoking Area, Disabled Facilities

162 The Rising Sun Inn
Woodland/Ashburton, Newton Abbot,
Devon TQ13 7JT
Tel: 01364 652544

Real Ales, Bar Food, Restaurant Menu,
Accommodation, No Smoking Area,
Disabled Facilities

163 The Royal Castle Hotel
11 The Quay, Dartmouth, Devon TQ6 9PS
Tel: 01803 833033

Real Ales, Bar Food, Restaurant Menu,
Accommodation, No Smoking Area,
Disabled Facilities

164 The Royal Oak
Higher Town, Malborough, Kingsbridge,
Devon TQ7 3RL
Tel: 01548 561481

Real Ales, Bar Food, Restaurant Menu,
No Smoking Area

165 Royal Oak Inn
Bigbury, Kingsbridge, Devon TQ7 4AP
Tel: 01548 810313

Real Ales, Bar Food, Restaurant Menu,
Accommodation, No Smoking Area

166 The Royal Oak Inn
5 East St, Ashburton, Newton Abbot,
Devon TQ13 7AD
Tel: 01364 652444

Real Ales, Bar Food, Restaurant Menu

174 The Ship Inn

Queen Street, Teignmouth, Devon TQ14 8BY
☎ 01676 772674 / 772061

Real Ales, Bar Food, Restaurant Menu, No Smoking Area, Disabled Facilities

☞ Tucked away by the water's edge in Teignmouth

🍺 Rotating choice

🍴 12-2.30 & 6-9.30

⛴ Seating area by the water

💳 Major cards accepted

🕐 11-12

🏛 All the attractions of Teignmouth; Shaldon Wildlife Trust 1 mile, Dawlish 2½ miles, Newton Abbot 5 miles

The Ship Inn is a much-loved pub right on the front in the resort of Teignmouth. With its two miles of beaches, a splendid promenade and a classic pier, Teignmouth

a ship, well-kept ales and a good choice of wines are available to enjoy on their own or to accompany a snack or a meal. Among the excellent home-cooked dishes, the pub is best known for its seafood specials, but the menu extends to many other choices, and almost all the ingredients are locally caught or locally sourced. Some dishes are plain and simple, others more elaborate: a good example is plaice, served grilled with lemon butter or stuffed with scallops and crab, topped with prawns. Other typical offerings could be Cajun chicken, pan-fried red mullet and grilled lamb chops with a delicious redcurrant gravy.

The Ship, well known to locals and families, is well worth seeking out at the water's edge, and once found will soon find its way onto the itineraries of visitors from outside the region. The pub is open from 11 every day, with food served every lunchtime and evening.

deserves its popularity, and The Ship, which backs right onto the river, also deserves its reputation as a great place to relax with a drink and something to eat.

When the weather is fine there are often more people sitting outside than in, watching the activity on the water and drinking in the terrific views across the estuary. Tenant Kim Jones and The Ship's crew are always ready with a smile, and the atmosphere here is always friendly and welcoming, even at the busiest times. In the bar, on two levels like two decks of

167 Royal Seven Stars

The Plains, Totnes, Devon TQ9 5DD
Tel: 01803 862125

Real Ales, Bar Food, Restaurant Menu, Accommodation, No Smoking Area, Disabled Facilities

168 The Royal Standard

Fore St, Shaldon, Teignmouth, Devon TQ14 0DZ
Tel: 01626 872442

Real Ales, Bar Food, Restaurant Menu, Accommodation, No Smoking Area, Disabled Facilities

169 The Saracens Head

Fairfield Terrace, Newton Abbot, Devon TQ12 2LH
Tel: 01626 365430

Real Ales

170 The Sea Trout Inn

Staverton, Totnes, Devon TQ6 0AA
Tel: 01803 762258

Real Ales, Bar Food, Restaurant Menu,
Accommodation, No Smoking Area,
Disabled Facilities

See panel below

171 The Seale Arms

10 Victoria Rd, Dartmouth, Devon TQ6 9SA
Tel: 01803 832719

Real Ales, Bar Food, Accommodation,
No Smoking Area, Disabled Facilities

172 The Seven Stars

Smith St, Dartmouth, Devon TQ6 9QR
Tel: 01803 832575

Real Ales, Bar Food, Restaurant Menu,
Accommodation, No Smoking Area

173 Ship In Dock

Ridge Hill, Dartmouth, Devon TQ6 9PE
Tel: 01803 835916

Real Ales, Bar Food

174 Ship Inn

Queen St, Teignmouth, Devon TQ14 8BY
Tel: 01626 772674

Real Ales, Bar Food, Restaurant Menu,
No Smoking Area, Disabled Facilities

See panel opposite

170 The Sea Trout Inn

Staverton, nr Totnes, Devon TQ9 6PA

☎ 01803 762274   ⊕ www.seatroutinn.com

**Real Ales, Bar Food, Restaurant Menu,
Accommodation, No Smoking Area,
Disabled Facilities**

☞ Close to the church in Staverton, 3 miles N of Totnes off the A384

🍺 Selection

🍴 Bar and restaurant menus L & D

🛏 10 rooms

⚓ Garden, car park

💳 Major cards accepted

🕐 L & D

🏛 Totnes 3 miles

Close to the village church in the delightful rural surroundings of the tranquil Dart Valley, the **Sea Trout Inn** has accurately been described as most people's idea of the idyllic Devon inn. Owners Nick and Nicky Brookland are charming hosts, and visitors are assured of a friendly welcome, superb service, comfortable accommodation and some of the best food in the region. The ten pretty, cottage-style twin or double bedrooms offer abundant character and comfort, and the top-of-the-range four-poster room has French windows that open onto the garden. Guests and non-residents may choose to eat in the elegant restaurant, in the relaxing surroundings of the bars, or even, on warm summer days, outside on the patio. Wherever they choose they will be enjoy the finest local produce carefully cooked and attractively presented.

175 The Ship Inn

Ugborough, Ivybridge, Devon PL21 0NS
Tel: 01752 892565

Real Ales, Restaurant Menu, No Smoking Area,
Disabled Facilities

176 The Ship Inn

9 Wolborough St, Newton Abbot, Devon TQ12 1JR
Tel: 01626 353409

Bar Food, No Smoking Area, Disabled Facilities

177 The Ship Inn

Higher St, Kingswear, Dartmouth, Devon TQ6 0AG
Tel: 01803 752348

Real Ales, Restaurant Menu, No Smoking Area

178 The Silent Whistle

34 St. Lawrence Lane, Ashburton, Newton Abbot,
Devon TQ13 7DD
Tel: 01364 654700

Real Ales, Bar Food, No Smoking Area

179 The Skipper Inn

57 Drew St, Brixham, Devon TQ5 9LA
Tel: 01803 855785

Real Ales, Bar Food, Restaurant Menu,
No Smoking Area, Disabled Facilities

180 Sloop Inn

Bantham, Kingsbridge, Devon TQ7 3AJ
Tel: 01548 560215

Real Ales, Bar Food, Restaurant Menu,
Accommodation, No Smoking Area

181 Smugglers Haunt Hotel

Church Hill East, Brixham, Devon TQ5 8HH
Tel: 01803 853050

Real Ales, Bar Food, Restaurant Menu,
Accommodation, No Smoking Area

See panel adjacent

182 The Smugglers Inn

Steamer Quay Rd, Totnes, Devon TQ9 5AL
Tel: 01803 863877

Real Ales, Bar Food, Restaurant Menu,
No Smoking Area

183 Soar Mill Cove Hotel

Malborough, Kingsbridge, Devon TQ7 3DS
Tel: 01548 561566

Real Ales, Bar Food, Restaurant Menu,
Accommodation, No Smoking Area,
Disabled Facilities

184 The Sportsmans Arms

Blackawton, Totnes, Devon TQ9 7DE
Tel: 01803 712231

Real Ales, Bar Food, Restaurant Menu,
No Smoking Area

185 The Sportsmans Inn

Exeter Rd, Ivybridge, Devon PL21 0BQ
Tel: 01752 892280

Real Ales, Bar Food, Restaurant Menu,
Accommodation, No Smoking Area,
Disabled Facilities

see panel opposite

181 The Smugglers Haunt Hotel

Church Hill, Brixham, Devon TQ5 8HH
☎ 01803 853050   🌐 www.smugglers-haunt-hotel.co.uk

**Real Ales, Bar Food, Restaurant Menu,
Accommodation, No Smoking Area**

- 400 yards from the harbour in Brixham
- 6.30-9.30 daily, also 12-2 Fri, Sat & Sun
- 14 en suite rooms
- Major cards accepted
- Restaurant and residents licence only
- Harbour 400 yards, Torquay 5 miles

The Ruffell family's **Smugglers Haunt Hotel** stands in the centre of Brixham an easy stroll from the harbour. Bar and restaurant menus make very good use of local produce, including fish from the daily market on the quay. The 14 guest bedrooms, all en suite, comprise single, twin and family rooms. They can be booked on a B&B or Dinner B&B basis.

185 The Sportsmans Inn & Ivybridge Hotel

Exeter Road, Ivybridge, Devon PL21 0BQ

☎ 01752 892280   🌐 www.thesportsmansinn.co.uk

Real Ales, Bar Food, Restaurant Menu,
Accommodation, No Smoking Area,
Disabled Facilities

- ☛ On the edge of town off the A38 Exeter-Plymouth road
- 🍺 Bass and guests
- 🍴 11.30-2.30 & 5-9.30 (all day Sat & Sun)
- 🛏 14 en suite rooms
- 🚗 Beer garden, car park
- 💳 Major cards accepted
- 🕐 11-11 (Sun 12-.10.30)
- 🏛 Two Moors Way; Butterdon Hill 1 mile,

Close to the A38 at the gateway to Dartmoor, the **Sportsmans Inn & Ivybridge Hotel** is open all year for food, drink and accommodation. Resident owners Bill and Doh Hibbert and their staff guarantee that the atmosphere at their 17th century inn – originally three cottages – is always homely and friendly, and the location makes it an ideal place to pause for refreshment or to stay for a longer break. Fourteen en suite bedrooms, all double glazed, with en suite or private bathroom, come in a variety of sizes, and all are equipped with telephone, television, hot drink facilities and hairdryers. The bar is open all day every day (four real ales always on tap), and food on a nicely varied menu is served every lunchtime and evening and all day Saturday and Sunday. A roast is added to the menu for Sunday lunch, and Sunday evening is Curry Night.

186 The Sprat & Mackerel

23-24 The Quay, Brixham, Devon TQ5 8AW
Tel: 01803 883357

Real Ales, Restaurant Menu, Disabled Facilities

See panel on page 74

187 The Start Bay Inn

Torcross, Kingsbridge, Devon TQ7 2TQ
Tel: 01548 580553

Real Ales, Bar Food, No Smoking Area

188 Steam Packet Inn

Fore St, Kingswear, Dartmouth, Devon TQ6 0AD
Tel: 01803 752208

Real Ales

189 Steam Packet Inn

St Peters Quay, Totnes, Devon TQ9 5EW
Tel: 01803 863880

Real Ales, Bar Food, Restaurant Menu,
Accommodation, No Smoking Area,
Disabled Facilities

190 Stoke Lodge Hotel

Cinders Lane, Stoke Fleming, Dartmouth,
Devon TQ6 0RA
Tel: 01803 770523

Real Ales, Bar Food, Restaurant Menu,
Accommodation, No Smoking Area

191 Striker Fort Xtra

Courtenay Place, Teignmouth, Devon TQ14 8AY
Tel: 01626 772348

Real Ales, Bar Food, Restaurant Menu

192 Sun Inn

1 Church St, Buckfastleigh, Devon TQ11 0BD
Tel: 01364 642397

Real Ales

193 The Swan Inn

4 Highweek St, Newton Abbot,
Devon TQ12 1TG
Tel: 01626 365056

Real Ales

186 The Sprat & Mackerel

24 The Quay, Brixham, Devon TQ5 8AW
☎ 01803 883357

Real Ales, Restaurant Menu, Disabled Facilities

☛ Across the road from the harbour at Brixham

🍺 Marston Pedigree

🍴 12-3 & 6-9

🎵 Live music Fri & Sat in season

⛱ Small seating area at front

🕐 All day

🏛 Paignton 4 miles, Kingswear 3 miles, Dartmouth 5 miles

The setting, just across the road from the harbour at Brixham, is just one of the attractions of the **Sprat & Mackerel**. Leaseholders Tony and Wendy have won many friends in this, their first venture into the licensed trade, and the charming 17th century inn is a popular choice with the locals and with the visitors who visit this part of the world in the summer. The name and the location make it entirely appropriate that fish dishes are the main speciality, but the menus and daily specials offer plenty of choice for everyone, including platters to share and a mini-club menu for children. Booking is advisable throughout the summer season. The inn is open all day for drinks, with Marston Pedigree the resident cask ale. On most Friday and Saturday evenings in summer live music sessions start at about 9 o'clock.

203 The Tradesmans Arms

Stokenham, nr Kingsbridge, Devon TQ7 2SZ
☎ 01548 580313 🌐 www.thetradesmansarms.com

Real Ales, Bar Food, No Smoking Area

☛ In Stokenham, 200 yards from the A379 5 miles E of Kingsbridge

🍺 Brakspear, South Hams

🍴 12-2.30 & 7-9.30 (not Mon eve)

⛱ Car park

💳 Major cards except Amex, Diners

🕐 L & D (all day Sun)

🏛 Kingsbridge 5 miles, Salcombe 6 miles, Dartmouth 8 miles

A detour of a few seconds from the A379 brings visitors to the **Tradesmans Arms**, a picture-postcard inn that has served the local community for many centuries. Part thatched, part tile-roofed, the inn is festooned with a wonderful colourful show of flowers in spring and summer, and the bar and eating areas are no less attractive. Gnarled black beams and country-style furniture assist the appealing old-world ambience, and affable hosts Nick and Rebecca make everyone very welcome, young or old, familiar faces or new. The dishes on the printed menu and specials board, served every session except Monday evening, highlight locally sourced produce and are complemented by fine wines and five real ales, including a bitter from the local South Hams Brewery.

194 The Tally Ho Inn

Littlehempston, Totnes, Devon TQ9 6NF
Tel: 01803 862316

Real Ales, Bar Food, Restaurant Menu,
Accommodation

195 Tavistock Inn

Poundsgate, Newton Abbot, Devon TQ13 7NY
Tel: 01364 631251

Real Ales, Bar Food, Restaurant Menu,
No Smoking Area

196 The Teign Brewery Inn

Teign St, Teignmouth, Devon TQ14 8EG
Tel: 01626 772684

Disabled Facilities

197 The Thatched Tavern

Steep Hill , Maidencombe, Torquay,
Devon TQ1 4TS
Tel: 01803 329155

Real Ales, Bar Food, Restaurant Menu,
No Smoking Area

198 Three Elms

28 Drew St, Brixham, Devon TQ5 9JU
Tel: 01803 852009

Real Ales, Bar Food

199 Thurlestone Hotel

Thurlestone, Kingsbridge, Devon TQ7 3NN
Tel: 01548 560382

Real Ales, Bar Food, Restaurant Menu,
Accommodation, No Smoking Area,
Disabled Facilities

200 Tom Cobley

Foxhole Rd, Paignton, Devon TQ3 3SS
Tel: 01803 403406

Bar Food, Restaurant Menu, No Smoking Area

201 The Torcross Tavern

Torcross, Kingsbridge, Devon TQ7 2TQ
Tel: 01548 580669

Real Ales, Bar Food, No Smoking Area,
Disabled Facilities

202 The Tower Inn

Slapton, Kingsbridge, Devon TQ7 2PN
Tel: 01548 580216

Real Ales, Bar Food, Restaurant Menu,
Accommodation, No Smoking Area

203 The Tradesmans Arms

Stokenham, Kingsbridge, Devon TQ7 2SZ
Tel: 01548 580313

Real Ales, Bar Food, No Smoking Area

See panel opposite

204 Tradesmens Arms

Scorriton, Buckfastleigh, Devon TQ11 0JB
Tel: 01364 631206

Real Ales, Bar Food, Restaurant Menu,
No Smoking Area

205 The Trawler

66 North Boundary Rd, Brixham, Devon TQ5 8LA
Tel: 01803 854062

Real Ales, Bar Food, Restaurant Menu,
No Smoking Area, Disabled Facilities

206 Two Mile Oak Inn

Two Mile Oak, Newton Abbot, Devon TQ12 6DF
Tel: 01803 812411

Real Ales, Bar Food, Restaurant Menu,
No Smoking Area

207 The Union Inn

6 East St, Newton Abbot, Devon TQ12 1AF
Tel: 01626 354775

Real Ales, Bar Food, Restaurant Menu,
Accommodation

208 The Union Inn

Denbury Green, Denbury, Newton Abbot,
Devon TQ12 6DQ
Tel: 01803 812595

Real Ales, Bar Food, No Smoking Area

209 Victoria Inn

77 North St, Ashburton, Newton Abbot,
Devon TQ13 7QH
Tel: 01364 652402

Real Ales, Bar Food, Restaurant Menu,
Accommodation, No Smoking Area,
Disabled Facilities

210 The Vigilance

5 Bolton St, Brixham, Devon TQ5 9DE
Tel: 01803 850489

Real Ales, Bar Food, Restaurant Menu,
No Smoking Area, Disabled Facilities

211 The Village Inn

Thurlstone, Kingsbridge, Devon TQ7 3NN
Tel: 01548 563525

Real Ales, Bar Food, Restaurant Menu,
No Smoking Area, Disabled Facilities

212 The Watermans Arms

Bow Bridge , Ashprington, Totnes,
Devon TQ9 7EG
Tel: 08703 305203

Real Ales, Bar Food, Restaurant Menu,
Accommodation, No Smoking Area

213 Watermans Arms

22 Chapel St, Buckfastleigh, Devon TQ11 0AQ
Tel: 01364 643200

Real Ales, Bar Food, No Smoking Area

214 Watermans Arms

Victoria St, Totnes, Devon TQ9 5EF
Tel: 01803 863525

Real Ales

215 Watermans Arms Inn

107 Drew St, Brixham, Devon TQ5 9LA
Tel: 01803 852028

Real Ales, Bar Food, Restaurant Menu,
No Smoking Area

216 Waterside Inn

126 Dartmouth Rd, Paignton, Devon TQ4 6ND
Tel: 01803 551113

Real Ales, Bar Food, Restaurant Menu,
No Smoking Area, Disabled Facilities

217 The Weary Ploughman Inn

Dartmouth Rd, Churston Ferrers, Brixham,
Devon TQ5 0LL
Tel: 01803 844702

Real Ales, Restaurant Menu, Accommodation,
No Smoking Area

218 Welcome Stranger Inn

Liverton, Newton Abbot, Devon TQ12 6JA
Tel: 01626 821224

Real Ales, Bar Food, Restaurant Menu,
Accommodation, No Smoking Area,
Disabled Facilities

219 Wellington Inn

Fore St, Ipplepen, Newton Abbot, Devon TQ12 5RH
Tel: 01803 814342

Real Ales, Bar Food, Restaurant Menu,
No Smoking Area, Disabled Facilities

220 Wetherspoon

34-42 Queen St, Newton Abbot,
Devon TQ12 2EW
Tel: 01626 323930

Real Ales, Bar Food, Restaurant Menu,
No Smoking Area, Disabled Facilities

221 The White Hart

2 Plymouth Rd, Buckfastleigh, Devon TQ11 0DA
Tel: 01364 642337

Real Ales

222 The White Hart

8 East St, Newton Abbot, Devon TQ12 1AG
Tel: 01626 363910

Real Ales, Bar Food, Accommodation

223 The Wild Goose

Combeinteignhead, Newton Abbot,
Devon TQ12 4RA
Tel: 01626 872241

Real Ales, Bar Food, No Smoking Area

224 The Willow Tree

Condor Way, Torquay, Devon TQ2 7TG
Tel: 01803 615245

Bar Food, Restaurant Menu, No Smoking Area

225 The Windjammer

Victoria Rd, Dartmouth, Devon TQ6 9RT
Tel: 01803 832228

Real Ales, Bar Food

226 The Woodpecker Inn

The Woodpecker, South Brent, Devon TQ10 9ES
Tel: 01364 72125

Real Ales, Bar Food, Restaurant Menu,
No Smoking Area, Disabled Facilities

See panel below

227 The Yard Arms

Beach Approach, Brixham, Devon TQ5 8JL
Tel: 01803 858266

Real Ales, Bar Food, Restaurant Menu,
No Smoking Area, Disabled Facilities

228 Ye Olde Cider Bar

99 East St, Newton Abbot, Devon TQ12 2LD
Tel: 01626 354221

No Smoking Area

229 Ye Olde Jolly Sailor Inn

46 Northumberland Place, Teignmouth,
Devon TQ14 8DE
Tel: 01626 772864

Real Ales

230 Ye Olde Smokey House

Vicarage Rd, Marldon, Paignton,
Devon TQ3 1NN
Tel: 01803 557630

Real Ales, Bar Food, Restaurant Menu

231 Ye Queens Arms

Dartington, Totnes, Devon TQ9 6NR
Tel: 01803 863210

Real Ales, Bar Food, Restaurant Menu,
No Smoking Area

226 The Woodpecker Inn

South Brent, Devon TQ10 9ES
☎ 01364 72125

**Real Ales, Bar Food, Restaurant Menu,
No Smoking Area, Disabled Facilities**

 Take the South Brent turn off the A38 and follow minor roads

 Local ales

12-9

 Garden, car park

 Major cards accepted

12-11

 Ivybridge 5 miles

Back roads lead from the South Brent turn-off from the A38 to the **Woodpecker Inn**. The exterior of this 18th century building is very distinctive, with an overhanging tile-fronted storey above its porticoed entrance. The interior has some equally notable features, including modern brick pillars and a circular rough stone hearth. In this atmospheric setting

Christine and Robert Mitchell and their staff put the smiles on the faces of their many regular customers and visitors to the area with a fine choice of superb dishes on the printed menu and the several specials boards. Door wedge sandwiches provide substantial snacks, while typical main courses might be sea bass and mussels in a warm lemon cream, liver & bacon on a bed of rocket and spinach mash, Thai chicken curry and, for dessert, a luscious chocolate, rum and raisin terrine. News of the quality of the cooking has spread quickly, so booking is always advisable, particularly in the summer season.

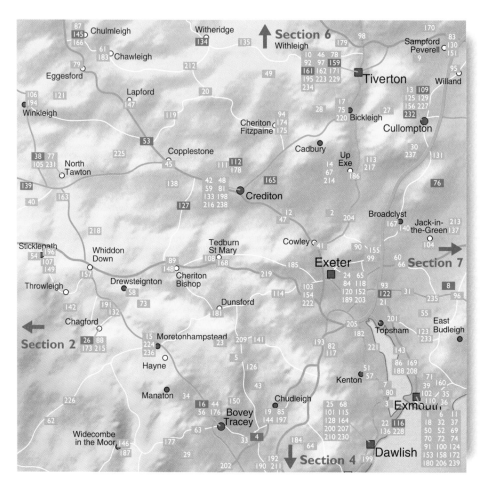

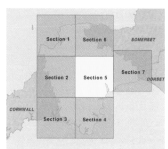

11	Pub or Inn Reference Number	- Detailed Information
12	Pub or Inn Reference Number	- Summary Entry
⬤ ⬛	Place of interest mentioned in the chapter introduction	

EXETER AND CENTRAL DEVON

The city of Exeter, which dominates the valley of the River Exe, marks the farthest point west reached by the Romans, and the Valley heads north in wonderful countryside, with Tiverton the only town of any size. This area also takes in the eastern part of Dartmoor, with Bovey Tracey on its very edge, and the coast below Exmouth, with Dawlish and Teignmouth at the start of the coastline known as the English Riviera.

Bickleigh

A charming place of thatched cottages and manicured gardens in a beautiful riverside setting. **Bickleigh Mill** is now a craft centre and rare breeds farm, while across the river stands the moated **Bickleigh Castle**, whose interior contains some excellent Tudor furniture, fine oil paintings and a Civil War armoury.

Bickleigh

Bovey Tracey

The river on which Bovey Tracey stands and the de Tracey family who were given the manor by William the Conqueror provided the name of this ancient market town. Among the places of interest are **Riverside Mill** – a craft centre and museum, the **House of Marbles and Teign Valley Glass**, **Cardew Teapottery** and the National Trust's **Parke**, headquarters of the Dartmoor National Park Authority.

Broadclyst

Just north of the village lies the large estate of **Killerton**, a grand 18th century manor house. The marvellous grounds include many rare trees and plants, two preserved workers' cottages and the **Dolbury Iron Age Hill Fort**.

Cadbury

On a hilltop 700 feet above sea level, **Cadbury Castle** is an Iron Age hill fort commanding some of the finest views in the whole county. Nearby **Fursdon House** contains many fascinating memorabilia, including 18th century costumes and textiles and a letter written by Charles I during the Civil War.

Chudleigh

William of Orange stayed here on his way to London, and the new king addressed the townsfolk from an upstairs window of the coaching inn. Nearby **Ugbrooke House**, set in superb gardens, is noted for its portraits by Lely, Chippendale furniture, Chinese porcelain and military uniforms.

Crediton

Nestling between two hills on the western bank of the River Creedy, Crediton was once famous for its wool industry and its cattle market. There were also tanneries here, which led to the town becoming associated with the manufacture of shoes and boots. The most important building here is the grand cathedral-like **Church of the Holy Cross**, a red sandstone building whose interior is filled with remarkable monuments. Part of the stained glass depicts the life of St Boniface, who was born (as Winfrith) in Crediton. Crediton railway station is on the famous Tarka Line.

Cullompton

Cullompton's crowning glory is the **Church of St Andrew**, a wonderful example of English Perpendicular Gothic.

Dawlish

A pretty seaside resort with one of the safest beaches in England. It has the unusual feature of a railway line that separates the town from the seafront. Jane Austen and

Charles Dickens are among the distinguished visitors to the town, which attracts today's tourists with its beaches, its elegant buildings and a **Museum** with a Victorian parlour and collections of china, prints, industrial tools, toys and early surgical instruments. A couple of miles up the coast lies **Dawlish Warren**, a mile-long spit of sand that includes a nature reserve with more than 450 species of flowers and plants.

Drewsteington

An appealing village of thatched cottages and a medieval church by the square. The village overlooks the well-known beauty spot of **Fingle Bridge**, a 400-year-old structure over the River Teign. Nearby **Castle Drogo**, though medieval in appearance, was in fact built between 1911 and 1930 to an Edwin Lutyens design for the tea baron Julius Drew, who founded the Home & Colonial Stores.

East Budleigh

Sir Walter Raleigh's family pew can be seen in **All Saints Church**, along with 16th century bench ends carved by local artisans. To the northwest lie **Bicton Park Botanical Gardens**, one of the country's most magnificent historic gardens. The Italian Garden was created in the style of Le Notre.

Exeter

The regional capital of the Southwest, Exeter is a lively, thriving city with a majestic **Norman Cathedral**, many other fine old buildings, the **Royal Albert Memorial Museum** and a history stretching back to Roman times. **St Nicholas' Priory**, the **Guildhall**, the **Custom House** and **Quay House Visitor Centre**, and the **University** buildings and gardens are all well worth a visit, but the most unusual attraction must be the **Underground Passages**, where guided tours show how water was brought to the city.

Exmouth

Often called the 'Bath of the West', Exmouth developed for the cream of society, and both Lady Byron and Lady Nelson stayed in the **Beacon**, an elegant Georgian terrace overlooking the esplanade. Among other interesting buildings are **Nelson House**, the **Assembly Rooms**, the **Museum** (housed in the old town council stables) and the unique 16-sided **A La Ronde**, which has been described as the most unusual house in Britain.

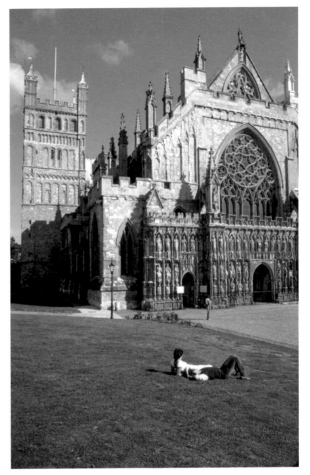

Exeter Cathedral

Kenton

Kenton is famed for its glorious 14th century **Church**, whose tower is decorated with a wonderful assortment of ornate carvings. To the east of the village stands **Powderham Castle**, set in one of the finest deer parks in Devon. The Castle, home to the Courtney family, Earls of Devon, since 1390, houses many family portraits, including some by Devon-born Sir Joshua Reynolds.

Manaton

From the porch of the 15th century village church can be seen the granite stack of **Bowerman's Nose**, while to the west lies **Grimspound**, the most impressive of Dartmoor's surviving Bronze Age Settlements. The area is bleak and moody, an atmosphere that recommended itself to Sir Arthur Conan Doyle as the setting for *The Hound of the Baskervilles*. To the south of Manaton, **Becky Falls Moorland Park** is one of the most beautiful places in the county.

Moretonhampstead

An attractive little hilltop town with a 15th century granite church and a row of unusual thatched, arcaded almshouses built in 1639. Two miles to the west lies the popular family attraction of the **Miniature Pony and Animal Farm**.

Sticklepath

A neat little village on the edge of Dartmoor that was once a busy industrial centre producing tools for agriculture and mining. Regular demonstrations of this industry are held in the **Finch Foundry Working Museum**.

Tiverton

The town developed round its **Castle**, built in 1106 and rebuilt and enlarged 200 years later. There's much in the town to interest the visitor, including two fine churches, **Blundell's School** and the **Tiverton Museum of Mid-Devon Life**. A couple of miles north lies **Knightshayes**, a striking Victorian Gothic mansion surrounded by superb gardens, parkland and woodland.

Topsham

Once famous for its shipbuilding industry, Topsham was at one time a larger port than Exeter, and its rich maritime heritage is reflected in the many fine 17th and 18th century merchant's houses, some of them built in the distinctive Dutch style. A group

Knightshayes Court, Tiverton

of such buildings near the Quay houses **Topsham Museum**.

Widecombe-in-the-Moor

The grand old **Church of St Pancras**, often called the Cathedral of the Moors, was built with funds raised by the tin miners of the 14th century. Its chief glory is its massive 120ft granite tower. The annual **Widecombe Fair** is known the world over for the song that tells the story of Uncle Tom Cobbleigh, his friends and his old grey mare on their way to the Fair.

Winkleigh

A top attraction in this hilltop village is the **Winkleigh Cider Company**, where cider has been produced from locally grown apples since 1916.

Widecombe-in-the-Moor

1 | 11a Bar

11A Church St, Exmouth, Devon EX8 1PE
Tel: 01395 223195

Real Ales, Bar Food, No Smoking Area

2 | The Agricultural Inn

Brampford Speke, Exeter, Devon EX5 5DP
Tel: 01392 841591

Real Ales, Bar Food, Restaurant Menu,
No Smoking Area

3 | The Anchor Inn

Cockwood, Starcross, Exeter, Devon EX6 8RA
Tel: 01626 890203

Real Ales, Bar Food, Restaurant Menu,
No Smoking Area

4 | The Anchor Inn

Plymouth Rd, Chudleigh Knighton, Chudleigh,
Devon TQ13 0EN
Tel: 01626 853123

Real Ales, Bar Food

See panel below

5 | Artichoke Inn

Village Rd, Christow, Exeter, Devon EX6 7NF
Tel: 01647 252387

Real Ales, Bar Food, Restaurant Menu,
No Smoking Area, Disabled Facilities

6 | Ashton Court Hotel

5-6 Louisa Terrace, Exmouth, Devon EX8 2AQ
Tel: 01395 263002

Real Ales, Bar Food, Restaurant Menu,
Accommodation, Disabled Facilities

7 | Atmospheric Railway Inn

The Strand, Starcross, Exeter, Devon EX6 8PA
Tel: 01626 890335

Real Ales

8 | Aylesbeare Inn

Village Way, Aylesbeare, Exeter, Devon EX5 2BX
Tel: 01395 232524

Real Ales, Bar Food, Restaurant Menu,
No Smoking Area

See panel opposite

---

4 | The Anchor

Chudleigh Knighton, Devon TQ13 0EN
☎ 01626 853123

Real Ales, Bar Food

- On the B3344, just off the A38 between Chudleigh and Coldeast
- Doom Bar, Courage
- 12-11 (Indian dishes a speciality)
- Quiz Friday
- 12-11
- Nature Reserves 1 mile and 2 miles, Bovey Tracey 1 mile, Ugbrooke House 2 miles, Newton Abbot 4 miles

Starting life many centuries ago as a row of cottages, the Anchor is now a cosy country inn that's equally popular with the locals and with the many tourists who pass this way throughout the year. Landlord Geoff Bailey is the star of the show, and the whole place has a natural, lived-in feel that makes every visit a delight. Sharps Doom Bar and Courage Best and Directors are on tap, and bar food both traditional and exotic is served throughout opening times. Geoff is a dab hand at Indian dishes, which can be enjoyed on the premises or to take away. Pool and darts are the favourite pub games, and the pub quiz starts at 9 o'clock every Friday night.

8 The Aylesbeare Inn

Village Way, Aylesbeare, nr Exeter,
Devon EX5 2BX

☎ 01395 232524

**Real Ales, Bar Food, Restaurant Menu,
No Smoking Area**

- ☛ On the A3052 Exeter-Sidmouth road, close to the airport. Leave the M5 at J30
- 🍺 Doom Bar, Broadside
- 🍴 L & D; steak night Thursday
- 🎵 Quiz one Sunday a month
- 🚗 Car park
- 💳 Major cards accepted
- 🕐 12-3 & 5.30-11 (all day Sat)
- 🏛 Exeter 3 miles, Crealy Adventure Park 2 miles

The Aylesbeare Inn is a fine-looking pub in the village of the same name, located on the A3052 Exeter to Sidmouth road. The interior is everything an English country pub should be, with a winning old-world look and feel, and tenants Peter and Margaret Weatherill have made many friends in their time here. Peter is the ale expert (well-kept Doom Bar and Broadside among the choices on tap), while Margaret is the star in the kitchen. Her repertoire is truly amazing, from bar snacks hot and cold and classics such as beer-battered cod or steak & kidney pie to daily changing fish specials (grey mullet, gurnard) and chicken Cordon Bleu. There's a 'grown-up' children's menu and desserts that you shouldn't even try to resist. Thursday is steak night. When the sun shines, the lawned garden is a delightful spot for all the family, with swings to keep the little ones happy.

9 The Barge

High St, Halberton, Tiverton, Devon EX16 7AG
Tel: 01884 820316

Real Ales, Bar Food, Restaurant Menu,
No Smoking Area

10 Barley Mow

Barrington St, Tiverton, Devon EX16 6QS
Tel: 01884 252028

Real Ales, Bar Food, Restaurant Menu,
No Smoking Area, Disabled Facilities

11 The Beacon Vaults

Beacon Hill, Exmouth, Devon EX8 1PB
Tel: 01395 272138

Real Ales, No Smoking Area

12 The Beer Engine

Newton St Cyres, Exeter, Devon EX5 5DA
Tel: 01392 851282

Real Ales, Bar Food, Restaurant Menu

13 The Bell Inn

20-22 Exeter Rd, Cullompton,
Devon EX15 1ED
Tel: 01884 35672

Real Ales, Bar Food, Restaurant Menu,
No Smoking Area, Disabled Facilities

14 The Bell Inn

The Berry, Thorverton, Exeter, Devon EX5 5NT
Tel: 01392 861421

Real Ales, Bar Food, Restaurant Menu,
No Smoking Area, Disabled Facilities

15 The Bell Inn

Cross St, Moretonhampstead, Newton Abbot,
Devon TQ13 8NL
Tel: 01647 440381

Real Ales, Bar Food

16 The Bell Inn

Town Hall Place, Bovey Tracey, Devon TQ13 9AA
☎ 01626 833495

Real Ales, Disabled Facilities

 Opposite the War Memorial at the top of town

 Selection

 3 rooms

 Patio

 12-3 & 5-11 (all day Sat & Sun)

🏛 The sights of Bovey Tracey; Ashburton 6 miles

A visit to the **Bell** will remind pub-lovers of how pubs used to be – pleasant, unpretentious surroundings, well-kept ales and a friendly welcome from behind the bar. That's the way hardworking tenants Keith and Sandra Cowie want it, and that's the way their regular customers like it. The frontage of this super little 16th century inn is bedecked with window boxes and hanging baskets, and inside, the bar is homely and inviting with tables and chairs spaced to best advantage for relaxing and unwinding with a drink. Outside is a pleasant, leafy courtyard. Right opposite the War Memorial at the top end of town, the Bell is a pleasant starting or finishing point for a walk around Bovey Tracey, and for guests wanting a longer break in this lovely old town the inn has three letting bedrooms with shared facilities.

---

16 The Bell Inn

Town Hall Place, Bovey Tracey, Newton Abbot,
Devon TQ13 9AA
Tel: 01626 833495

Real Ales, Disabled Facilities

See panel above

17 Bickleigh Cottage

Bickleigh, Tiverton, Devon EX16 8RJ
Tel: 01884 855230

Bar Food, Restaurant Menu, Accommodation,
No Smoking Area, Disabled Facilities

18 The Bicton Inn

5 Bicton St, Exmouth, Devon EX8 2RU
Tel: 01395 272589

Real Ales

19 Bishop Lacey Inn

Fore St, Chudleigh, Newton Abbot,
Devon TQ13 0HY
Tel: 01626 854585

Real Ales, Bar Food, Restaurant Menu,
No Smoking Area

20 Black Dog Inn

Black Dog Village, Black Dog, Crediton,
Devon EX17 4QS
Tel: 01884 860336

Real Ales, Bar Food, Restaurant Menu,
No Smoking Area

21 The Blue Ball Inn

Sandygate, Exeter, Devon EX2 7JL
Tel: 01392 873401

Real Ales, Bar Food, Restaurant Menu,
No Smoking Area, Disabled Facilities

22 The Boat House

Beach Way, Dawlish Warren, Dawlish,
Devon EX7 0NF
Tel: 01626 888899

Real Ales, Restaurant Menu, No Smoking Area,
Disabled Facilities

23 Bridford Inn

Bridford, Exeter, Devon EX6 7HT
Tel: 01647 252436

Real Ales, Bar Food, Restaurant Menu,
No Smoking Area

24 The Bridge Inn

Bridge Hill, Topsham, Exeter, Devon EX3 0QQ
Tel: 01392 873862

Real Ales, Bar Food, Restaurant Menu,
No Smoking Area, Disabled Facilities

25 Brunswick Arms

Brunswick Place, Dawlish, Devon EX7 9PB
Tel: 01626 862181

Real Ales, Bar Food

26 Bullers Arms

7 Mill St, Chagford, Newton Abbot,
Devon TQ13 8AW
Tel: 01647 432348

Real Ales, Bar Food, Restaurant Menu,
Accommodation, No Smoking Area

See panel below

27 The Butterleigh Inn

Butterleigh, Cullompton, Devon EX15 1PN
Tel: 01884 855407

Real Ales, Bar Food, Restaurant Menu,
Accommodation, No Smoking Area,
Disabled Facilities

28 The Cadleigh Arms

Cadleigh, Tiverton, Devon EX16 8HP
Tel: 01884 855238

Real Ales, Bar Food, No Smoking Area

29 Carpenters Arms

Ilsington, Newton Abbot, Devon TQ13 9RG
Tel: 01364 661215

Real Ales, Bar Food, Restaurant Menu,
No Smoking Area

26 The Bullers Arms

Mill Street, Chagford, Devon TQ13 8AW
☎ 01647 432348   ⊕ www.thebullersarms.co.uk

**Real Ales, Bar Food, Restaurant Menu,
Accommodation, No Smoking Area**

☛ Leave the A30 at Whiddon Down, then the
A382; turn off right to Chagford after 4 miles

🍸 Selection

🍴 12-2 & 6.30-9, Carvery service 12-6 Sunday

🛏 3 en suite rooms

⚒ Garden

💳 Major cards accepted

🕐 11-3 & 5-11 (all day Fri-Sun)

🏛 Dartmoor on the doorstep; Castle Drogo 2
miles, Spinster's Rock 3 miles

Maurice and Wendy Cox make everyone very welcome at the **Bullers Arms**, a fine old inn at the heart of the charming Devon town of Chagford. The interior of the inn, some which dates back to the 1700s, has been sympathetically updated whilst retaining many original features. Ceiling beams and a large stone fireplace enhance the traditional look within, and when the weather is kind the large, secluded beer garden is a perfect spot to enjoy a drink (including 2/3 real ales always on tap) and a snack or a meal. Maurice and Wendy are rapidly gaining an excellent reputation for good food, and the chalkboard menus provide a daily-changing choice of good-value favourites and vegetarian dishes. A Sunday carvery has now been added to enhance the menu with a choice of meats being offered, accompanied by a selection of fresh vegetables. Three en suite rooms offer a good base for discovering the delights of Dartmoor National Park.

38 The Copper Key Inn

Fore Street, North Tawton, Devon EX20 2ED
☎ 01837 82357

Real Ales, Bar Food, Restaurant Menu, Accommodation, No Smoking Area

- ☞ Off the A3072 6 miles NE of Okehampton
- 🍺 Rotating guests
- 🍴 12-10
- 🛏 3 rooms
- ♫ Live music Saturday evening
- ⛏ Garden; car park opposite
- 💳 Major cards except Amex
- 🕐 11-11 (Sun 12-10.30)
- 🏛 Tarka Trail nearby; Okehampton 6 miles

On the edge of the scattered community of North Tawton, the **Copper Key Inn** is a wonderful, traditional country hostelry dating back to the 16th century. Flower tubs and hanging baskets adorn the lovely thatch-roofed exterior, and the spacious beamed bar retains many of its original features, including open fires and old beams.

The inn is in the very capable hands of Penny and Arthur Bath, who took over the premises in 2000. They have made this splendid free house a friendly and popular meeting place for local residents, and an equally warm welcome awaits the many visitors to this very pleasant part of the world. Two real ales are always on tap in the bar, along with an excellent range of other draught and bottled beers, lagers and ciders.

Food is also an important part of the inn's business, and the printed menu and the daily-changing specials board is available every lunchtime and evening. Penny does most of the cooking, and visitors can enjoy her freshly prepared, appetising dishes either in the bar or in the more formal separate restaurant. Children are welcome, and the inn has a pretty lawned garden with a pets corner.

The Copper Key is also a delightful, civilised choice for a relaxing break in the country and a base for exploring North Tawton and the surrounding area. The inn has two single rooms and a double, and the day starts with a hearty Devon breakfast. This is great walking country, and the Tarka Trail passes close to the inn. The more energetic could for the vast open spaces of Dartmoor, including the mighty Yes Tor, which rises to more the 2,000 feet and is therefore officially a mountain. Attractions at nearby Okehampton, known as the 'Gateway to Dartmoor', include the imposing ruins of what was once the largest castle in Devon.

30 The Castle Hotel

Fore St, Bradninch, Exeter, Devon EX5 4NN
Tel: 01392 881378

Real Ales, Bar Food, Accommodation,
No Smoking Area, Disabled Facilities

31 The Cat & Fiddle Inn

Clyst St. Mary, Exeter, Devon EX5 1DP
Tel: 01392 873317

Real Ales, Bar Food, Restaurant Menu,
No Smoking Area, Disabled Facilities

32 Cavendish Hotel

11-12 Morton Crescent/The Espalanade, Exmouth,
Devon EX8 1BE
Tel: 01395 263305

Restaurant Menu, Accommodation,
No Smoking Area, Disabled Facilities

33 Claycutters Arms

Chudleigh Knighton, Chudleigh, Newton Abbot,
Devon TQ13 0EY
Tel: 01626 853345

Real Ales, Bar Food, Restaurant Menu,
No Smoking Area

34 Cleave Hotel

Lustleigh, Newton Abbot, Devon TQ13 9TJ
Tel: 01647 277223

Real Ales, Bar Food, Restaurant Menu

35 The Clinton Arms

Maer Lane, Littleham, Exmouth, Devon EX8 2RL
Tel: 01395 263781

Real Ales, Bar Food, Restaurant Menu,
No Smoking Area

36 The Clinton Arms

Littleham Village, Littleham, Exmouth,
Devon EX8 2RQ
Tel: 01395 264054

Real Ales, Bar Food, Restaurant Menu,
No Smoking Area, Disabled Facilities

37 The Clipper

33-34 The Strand, Exmouth, Devon EX8 1AQ
Tel: 01395 279879

Real Ales, Bar Food, Restaurant Menu,
No Smoking Area

38 The Copper Key Inn

Fore St, North Tawton, Devon EX20 2ED
Tel: 01837 82357

Real Ales, Bar Food, Restaurant Menu,
Accommodation, No Smoking Area

See panel opposite

39 The Country House Inn

174-176 Withycombe Village Rd, Exmouth, Devon
EX8 3BA
Tel: 01395 269873

Real Ales, Bar Food, Restaurant Menu,
No Smoking Area, Disabled Facilities

40 The Countryman

Sampford Courtenay, Okehampton,
Devon EX20 2SA
Tel: 01837 82206

Real Ales, Bar Food, Restaurant Menu,
No Smoking Area

41 Cowley Bridge Inn

Cowley Bridge Rd, Exeter, Devon EX4 5BX
Tel: 01392 274268

Real Ales, Bar Food, Disabled Facilities

42 The Crediton Inn

28a Mill St, Crediton, Devon EX17 1EZ
Tel: 01363 772882

Real Ales, Bar Food, No Smoking Area

43 The Cridford Inn

Trusham, Newton Abbot, Devon TQ13 0NR
Tel: 01626 853694

Real Ales, Bar Food, Restaurant Menu,
Accommodation, No Smoking Area,
Disabled Facilities

44 Cromwell Arms Hotel

Fore St, Bovey Tracey, Newton Abbot,
Devon TQ13 9AE
Tel: 01626 833473

Real Ales, Bar Food, Restaurant Menu,
Accommodation, No Smoking Area,
Disabled Facilities

45 The Cross Inn

Copplestone, Crediton, Devon EX17 5NH
Tel: 01363 84273

Real Ales, Bar Food, Restaurant Menu,
No Smoking Area, Disabled Facilities

46 The Cross Keys

30 Gold St, Tiverton, Devon EX16 6PY
Tel: 01884 250206

Bar Food, No Smoking Area

47 The Crown & Sceptre

Newton St. Cyres, Exeter, Devon EX5 5DA
Tel: 01392 851278

Real Ales, Bar Food, Restaurant Menu,
No Smoking Area, Disabled Facilities

48 The Crown Of Crediton

Exeter Rd, Crediton, Devon EX17 3BR
Tel: 01363 772889

Restaurant Menu

49 The Cruwys Arms

Pennymoor, Tiverton, Devon EX16 8LF
Tel: 01363 866662

Real Ales, Bar Food, Restaurant Menu,
No Smoking Area, Disabled Facilities

50 The Deer Leap

Esplanade, Exmouth, Devon EX8 2AZ
Tel: 01395 265030

Real Ales, Bar Food, Restaurant Menu,
No Smoking Area, Disabled Facilities

51 The Devon Arms

Fore St, Kenton, Exeter, Devon EX6 8LD
Tel: 01626 890213

Real Ales, Bar Food, Restaurant Menu,
Accommodation, No Smoking Area,
Disabled Facilities

52 Devoncourt Hotel

Douglas Avenue, Exmouth, Devon EX8 1PB
Tel: 01395 272277

Real Ales, Bar Food, Restaurant Menu,
Accommodation, No Smoking Area,
Disabled Facilities

53 The Devonshire Dumpling

Morchard Rd, Crediton, Devon EX17 5LP
Tel: 01363 85102

Real Ales, Bar Food, Restaurant Menu,
Accommodation, No Smoking Area,
Disabled Facilities

See panel below

53 The Devonshire Dumpling

Morchard Road, Copplestone, nr Crediton,
Devon EX17 5LP

☎ 01363 85102   ⊕ www.devonshiredumpling.com

**Real Ales, Bar Food, Restaurant Menu,
Accommodation, No Smoking Area,
Disabled Facilities**

- On the A377 Barnstaple road NW of Copplestone
- Lunchtime and evening (all day Sun)
- 3 rooms (more planned)
- Garden, car park
- Major cards accepted
- Lunchtime and evening (all day Sun)
- Crediton 5 miles

Gordon and Janet Robinson meet and greet visitors to the **Devonshire Dumpling**, a cheerful, friendly inn on the A377. The inn's name brings a smile to the faces of customers, and those smiles broaden as they enjoy the excellent home cooking. Excellent country inn accommodation comprises three en suite rooms, one with a four-poster bed. Morchard Road station on

54 The Devonshire Inn
Sticklepath, Okehampton, Devon EX20 2NW
Tel: 01837 840626

Real Ales, Bar Food, Accommodation,
Disabled Facilities

55 The Diggers Rest
Woodbury, Woodbury Salterton, Exeter,
Devon EX5 1PQ
Tel: 01395 232375

Real Ales, Bar Food, Restaurant Menu,
No Smoking Area, Disabled Facilities

56 Dolphin Hotel
Station Rd, Bovey Tracey, Newton Abbot,
Devon TQ13 9AL
Tel: 01626 832413

Real Ales, Bar Food, Restaurant Menu,
Accommodation, No Smoking Area,
Disabled Facilities

57 The Dolphin Inn
Fore St, Kenton, Exeter, Devon EX6 8LD
Tel: 01626 891371

Real Ales, Bar Food, No Smoking Area,
Disabled Facilities

58 The Drew Arms
Drewsteignton, Drewsteignton,
Devon TQ13 9TJ
Tel: 01647 281224

Real Ales, Bar Food, Restaurant Menu,
Accommodation, No Smoking Area,
Disabled Facilities

59 Duke of York
High St, Crediton, Devon EX17 3JS
Tel: 01363 776701

Real Ales

60 The Duke of York
Clyst Honiton, Exeter, Devon EX5 2NH
Tel: 01392 367855

Bar Food, Disabled Facilities

61 The Earl of Portsmouth
Chawleigh, Chulmleigh, Devon EX18 7HJ
Tel: 01769 580204

Real Ales, Bar Food, Restaurant Menu,
No Smoking Area, Disabled Facilities

62 East Dart Hotel
Postbridge, Yelverton, Devon PL20 6TJ
Tel: 01822 880213

Real Ales, Bar Food, Restaurant Menu,
Accommodation

63 Edgemoor Hotel
Bovey Tracey, Newton Abbot, Devon TQ13 9LE
Tel: 01626 832466

Real Ales, Bar Food, Restaurant Menu,
Accommodation, No Smoking Area,
Disabled Facilities

64 Elizabethan Inn
Luton, Chudleigh, Newton Abbot,
Devon TQ13 0BL
Tel: 01626 775425

Real Ales, Bar Food, Restaurant Menu,
No Smoking Area, Disabled Facilities

65 Exeter Inn
68 High St, Topsham, Exeter, Devon EX3 0DY
Tel: 01392 873131

Real Ales, Accommodation

66 Exeter Inn
Clyst Honiton, Exeter, Devon EX5 2NJ
Tel: 01392 367907

Bar Food

67 Exeter Inn
Bullen St, Thorverton, Exeter, Devon EX5 5NG
Tel: 01392 860206

Real Ales, Disabled Facilities

68 The Exeter Inn
Beach St, Dawlish, Devon EX7 9PN
Tel: 01626 865677

Real Ales, Bar Food, No Smoking Area

69 Exmouth Arms
21 Exeter Rd, Exmouth, Devon EX8 1PN
Tel: 01395 265292

Real Ales

70 The Famous Ship Inn
High St, Exmouth, Devon EX8 1NP
Tel: 01395 264440

Real Ales, Bar Food, Restaurant Menu

71 The Farmhouse Inn
Brixington Parade, Churchill Rd, Exmouth,
Devon EX8 4JS
Tel: 01395 278000

Real Ales, Bar Food, Restaurant Menu,
No Smoking Area, Disabled Facilities

72 Fat Jax
8 Victoria Rd, Exmouth, Devon EX8 1DL
Tel: 01395 225440

Real Ales, Bar Food

73 Fingle Bridge Inn
Drewsteignton, Exeter, Devon EX6 6PW
Tel: 01647 281287

Real Ales, Bar Food, No Smoking Area

74 First & Last Inn
10 Church St, Exmouth, Devon EX8 1PE
Tel: 01395 263275

Real Ales, Bar Food, Disabled Facilities

75 Fisherman's Cot Hotel
Bickleigh, Tiverton, Devon EX16 8RW
Tel: 01884 855237

Real Ales, Bar Food, Restaurant Menu,
Accommodation, No Smoking Area,
Disabled Facilities

76 Five Bells Inn
Clyst Hydon, Cullompton, Devon EX15 2NT
Tel: 01884 277288

Real Ales, Bar Food, Restaurant Menu,
No Smoking Area, Disabled Facilities

See panel below

76 The Five Bells
Clyst Hydon, nr Cullompton, Devon EX15 2NT
☎ 01884 277288   ⊕ www.fivebellsclysthydon.co.uk

**Real Ales, Bar Food, Restaurant Menu,
No Smoking Area, Disabled Facilities**

☛ From A30 at Fairmile take the B3176 through Talaton to Clyst Hydon. The inn is outside the village on the road to Clyst St Lawrence

🍺 Otter, Tawny

🍴 Lunchtime and evening

⚓ Garden. car park

💳 Major cards accepted

🕐 11.30-3 (Sun from 12) & 6.30-11 (Sun to 10.30)

🏆 Best steak pie in England' commendation

🏛 Cullompton 4 miles, Exeter 7 miles

Just outside Clyst Hydon on the road to Clyst St Lawrence, the **Five Bells** is well worth seeking out for its food, its ales and wines and its delightful, relaxed atmosphere. Owners Di and Roger are firmly committed to continuing the long tradition of hospitality and warmth that the 16th century thatched free house enjoys, and they have an equally friendly welcome for valued regular customers and new faces. The bars and restaurant areas are both charmingly traditional and elegant stylish, with beams, prints, copper and brasses, providing a perfect setting for enjoying a glass of locally brewed ale and a meal. The chalkboard menus tempt with an interesting selection of dishes, from chunky chicken and apricot terrine or bacon-wrapped scallops to baked plaice, liver & bacon and superb pies – fish, vegetarian and a steak pie recently declared among the best in England.

77 The Fountain Inn
Exeter St, North Tawton, Devon EX20 2HB
Tel: 01837 82551

Real Ales, Bar Food

78 The Four In Hand
23 Fore St, Tiverton, Devon EX16 6LZ
Tel: 01884 258930

Real Ales, Disabled Facilities

79 Fox & Hounds
Eggesford, Chulmleigh, Devon EX18 7JZ
Tel: 01769 580345

Real Ales, Bar Food, Restaurant Menu,
Accommodation, No Smoking Area,
Disabled Facilities

80 The Galleon Inn
The Strand, Starcross, Exeter, Devon EX6 8PR
Tel: 01626 890412

Real Ales, Bar Food, Restaurant Menu,
Accommodation, No Smoking Area,
Disabled Facilities

81 The General Sir Redvers Buller
40 High St, Crediton, Devon EX17 3JP
Tel: 01363 774381

Real Ales, Bar Food, Restaurant Menu,
No Smoking Area, Disabled Facilities

82 Gissons Arms
Kennford, Exeter, Devon EX6 7UW
Tel: 01392 832444

Real Ales, Bar Food, Restaurant Menu,
Accommodation, No Smoking Area

83 The Globe
16 Lower Town, Sampford Peverell, Tiverton, Devon
EX16 7BJ
Tel: 01884 821214

Real Ales, Bar Food, Restaurant Menu,
Accommodation, No Smoking Area,
Disabled Facilities

84 Globe Hotel
Fore St, Topsham, Exeter, Devon EX3 0HR
Tel: 01392 873471

Real Ales, Bar Food, Restaurant Menu,
Accommodation, No Smoking Area,
Disabled Facilities

85 The Globe Hotel
Fore St, Chudleigh, Newton Abbot,
Devon TQ13 0HT
Tel: 01626 853219

Real Ales

86 Globe Inn
The Strand, Lympstone, Exmouth,
Devon EX8 5EY
Tel: 01395 263166

Real Ales, Bar Food, Restaurant Menu,
No Smoking Area, Disabled Facilities

87 The Globe Inn
Church St, Chulmleigh, Devon EX18 7BU
Tel: 01769 580252

Real Ales, Bar Food, Disabled Facilities

88 The Globe Inn
9 High St, Chagford, Newton Abbot,
Devon TQ13 8AJ
Tel: 01647 433485

Real Ales, Bar Food, Restaurant Menu,
No Smoking Area

89 The Good Knight Inn
Cheriton Bishop, Exeter, Devon EX6 6JH
Tel: 01647 24227

Real Ales, Bar Food, Restaurant Menu

90 Great Western Hotel
St David'S Station Approach, Exeter,
Devon EX4 9RW
Tel: 01392 274039

Real Ales, Bar Food, Restaurant Menu,
Accommodation, No Smoking Area

91 The Grove
Esplanade, Exmouth, Devon EX8 1BJ
Tel: 01395 272101

Real Ales, Bar Food, Restaurant Menu,
No Smoking Area, Disabled Facilities

92 The Half Moon Inn
Fore St, Tiverton, Devon EX16 6LD
Tel: 01884 253543

Real Ales, Bar Food, Disabled Facilities

93 The Half Moon Inn
Clyst St. Mary, Exeter, Devon EX5 1BR
Tel: 01392 873515

Real Ales, Bar Food, Restaurant Menu,
Accommodation, No Smoking Area,
Disabled Facilities

94 Half Moon Inn
Cheriton Fitzpaine, Crediton, Devon EX17 4JW
Tel: 01363 866219

Real Ales, No Smoking Area

95 The Halfway House
Willand, Cullompton, Devon EX15 2RF
Tel: 01884 820258

Real Ales, Bar Food, No Smoking Area,
Disabled Facilities

96 Halfway Inn
Aylesbeare, Exeter, Devon EX5 2JP
Tel: 01395 232273

Real Ales, Bar Food, Restaurant Menu,
Accommodation, No Smoking Area

97 The Hare & Hounds
138 Chapel St, Tiverton, Devon EX16 6BZ
Tel: 01884 252013

Real Ales, Bar Food

98 Hartnoll Country House Hotel
Bolham Rd, Bolham, Tiverton, Devon EX16 7RA
Tel: 01884 252777

Real Ales, Bar Food, Restaurant Menu,
Accommodation, No Smoking Area,
Disabled Facilities

99 Heart of Oak
34 Main Rd, Pinhoe, Exeter, Devon EX4 8HS
Tel: 01392 467329

Real Ales, Bar Food, Restaurant Menu,
No Smoking Area, Disabled Facilities

100 The Heavitree
High St, Exmouth, Devon EX8 1NP
Tel: 01395 263640

Bar Food, No Smoking Area, Disabled Facilities

101 The Hole in the Wall
28 The Strand, Dawlish, Devon EX7 9PS
Tel: 01626 862132

Real Ales, Bar Food, Disabled Facilities

102 Holly Tree Inn
161 Withycombe Village Rd, Exmouth,
Devon EX8 3AN
Tel: 01395 273440

Real Ales, Bar Food, Restaurant Menu,
No Smoking Area, Disabled Facilities

103 The Huntsman Inn
2 High St, Ide, Exeter, Devon EX2 9RN
Tel: 01392 272779

Real Ales, Bar Food, Restaurant Menu,
No Smoking Area, Disabled Facilities

104 The Jack in the Green Inn
Rockbeare, Exeter, Devon EX5 2EE
Tel: 01404 822240

Real Ales, Bar Food, Restaurant Menu,
No Smoking Area, Disabled Facilities

105 Kayden House Hotel
High St, North Tawton, Devon EX20 2HF
Tel: 01837 82242

Bar Food, Restaurant Menu, Accommodation,
No Smoking Area

106 The Kings Arms
Fore St, Winkleigh, Devon EX19 8HQ
Tel: 01837 83384

Real Ales, Bar Food, Restaurant Menu,
No Smoking Area

107 The Kings Arms

South Zeal, Okehampton, Devon EX20 2JP
Tel: 01837 840300

Real Ales, Bar Food, Restaurant Menu,
No Smoking Area, Disabled Facilities

108 The Kings Arms Inn

Tedburn St. Mary, Exeter, Devon EX6 6EG
Tel: 01647 61224

Real Ales, Bar Food, Restaurant Menu,
Accommodation, No Smoking Area

109 The Kings Head

35 High St, Cullompton, Devon EX15 1AF
Tel: 01884 32418

Real Ales, Bar Food, Restaurant Menu,
No Smoking Area, Disabled Facilities

See panel below

109 The Kings Head

High Street, Cullompton, Devon EX15 1AF
☎ 01884 32418

**Real Ales, Bar Food, Restaurant Menu,
No Smoking Area, Disabled Facilities**

☛ On the main street of Cullompton, 5 miles SE
of Tiverton; leave M5 at J28

🍺 Otter

🍴 All day

🎵 Jam session Tuesday, karaoke Friday, live bands
Saturday

💳 Major cards accepted

🕐 11-11 (Sun 12-10.30); from 9 am after Nov '05

🏛 Church of St Andrew in Cullompton; Tiverton
5 miles

The cheerful, sunny tone set by the hanging
baskets outside the Kings Head is
continued inside this fine old inn. The popular,
convivial pub is open all day for eating and
drinking. Otter and a guest ale are on tap, and
highlights on the menu include a range of
speciality sausages. The inn has a smart
modern function room and a pleasant garden.

110 Knights Hotel

7 Stevenstone Rd, Exmouth, Devon EX8 2EP
Tel: 01395 224488

Restaurant Menu, Accommodation,
No Smoking Area, Disabled Facilities

111 The Laffinn Pig

1 Commercial Rd, Dawlish, Devon EX7 9HU
Tel: 01626 867979

Real Ales, Bar Food, Disabled Facilities

112 The Lamb Inn

Sandford, Crediton, Devon EX17 4LW
Tel: 01363 773676

Real Ales, Bar Food, Restaurant Menu,
No Smoking Area, Disabled Facilities

See panel on page 96

113 The Lamb Inn

Fore St, Silverton, Exeter, Devon EX5 4HZ
Tel: 01392 860272

Real Ales, Bar Food, Restaurant Menu,
No Smoking Area, Disabled Facilities

114 The Lamb Inn

Longdown, Exeter, Devon EX6 7SR
Tel: 01392 811711

Real Ales, Bar Food, Restaurant Menu,
Disabled Facilities

115 Lansdowne

8 Park Rd, Dawlish, Devon EX7 9LQ
Tel: 01626 863201

Real Ales, Bar Food, Disabled Facilities

116 Lee's Bar

12 Mount Pleasant Rd, Dawlish Warren, Dawlish,
Devon EX7 0NA
Tel: 01626 863344

Real Ales, Restaurant Menu, No Smoking Area,
Disabled Facilities

See panel on page 96

117 The Ley Arms

Kenn, Exeter, Devon EX6 7UW
Tel: 01392 832341

Real Ales, Bar Food, Restaurant Menu,
No Smoking Area, Disabled Facilities

The Lamb Inn

The Square, Sandford, nr Crediton,
Devon EX17 4LW

☎ 01363 773676

**Real Ales, Bar Food, Restaurant Menu,
No Smoking Area, Disabled Facilities**

☞ In the middle of Sandford, on minor roads 2 miles N of Crediton

🍺 Piston + guests

🍴 All day

🎵 'Open mike' last Friday of month, live music most weekends

⛱ Beer garden

💳 Major cards accepted

🕐 9am-11pm Mon-Fri, 11am-11pm Sat, 10.30am-10.30pm Sun

🏛 Crediton 2 miles, Exeter 7 miles

Stepping inside the 16th century **Lamb Inn** is taking a step back in time, with the low black-beamed ceilings and fires setting a delightfully traditional scene. By contrast, modern fresh food is served all day every day, made mostly with locally sourced ingredients, often organic. There's space aplenty in the rambling bar areas, and tables and chairs are also set out in the beer garden to take advantage of balmy Devon days. Visitors can eat anywhere inside or out. Various events enliven most weekends, and on the last Friday of each month inhibitions are cast aside on 'open mike night. The Lamb with its friendly and welcoming environment is very much at the heart of the local community in and around the village of Sandford, which is easily reached along minor roads from nearby Crediton.

116 Lee's Bar

Mount Pleasant Road, Dawlish Warren,
Devon EX7 0NE

☎ 01626 863344

**Real Ales, Restaurant Menu, No Smoking Area,
Disabled Facilities**

☞ 2 miles up the coast from Dawlish

🍺 Otter + guests

🍴 5-10 (Sun 12.30-3.30)

⛱ Terrace

🕐 12-11 (from 5 in winter)

🏛 Nature Reserve and Amusement Park nearby

Lee's Bar, once purely a restaurant, is now a well-liked, well-located pub serving a good range of drinks and pub grub. Open all year round, Lee's does a roaring trade in the summer months, being close to popular resorts, the sea and an extensive amusement centre. It's also a favourite with the locals, and Gloria and Nigel have made many friends in their time here. Gloria is at the helm in the kitchen, producing a good choice of snacks and full meals served from 5 o'clock Monday to Saturday. On Sunday, the carvery, which functions from 12.30 to 3.30, is a real winner. There's plenty of floor and table space in the bar, and the picnic benches set out on the terrace are always in demand when the sun shines.

118 The Lighter Inn
Fore St, Topsham, Exeter, Devon EX3 0HZ
Tel: 01392 875439

Real Ales, Bar Food, Restaurant Menu,
No Smoking Area, Disabled Facilities

119 The London Inn
Morchard Bishop, Crediton, Devon EX17 6NW
Tel: 01363 877222

Real Ales, Bar Food, Restaurant Menu,
No Smoking Area, Disabled Facilities

120 The Lord Nelson Inn
High St, Topsham, Exeter, Devon EX3 0DU
Tel: 01392 873314

Real Ales, Bar Food, Restaurant Menu,
No Smoking Area

121 The Lymington Arms
Lama Cross, Wembworthy, Devon EX18 7SA
Tel: 01837 83572

Real Ales, Bar Food, Restaurant Menu,
Accommodation, No Smoking Area,
Disabled Facilities

122 The Maltsters Arms
Clyst St. Mary, Exeter, Devon EX5 1BL
Tel: 01392 873445

Real Ales, Bar Food, Restaurant Menu

See panel below

123 The Maltsters Arms
Woodbury, Exeter, Devon EX5 1LN
Tel: 01395 232218

Real Ales, Bar Food, Restaurant Menu

124 The Manor Hotel
The Beacon, Exmouth, Devon EX8 2AG
Tel: 01395 274477

Real Ales, Bar Food, Restaurant Menu,
Accommodation, No Smoking Area

125 Manor House Hotel
2-4 Fore St, Cullompton, Devon EX15 1JL
Tel: 01884 32281

Bar Food, Restaurant Menu, Accommodation,
No Smoking Area, Disabled Facilities

---

122 The Maltsters
Clyst St Mary, nr Exeter, Devon EX5 1BL
☎ 01392 873445

Real Ales, Bar Food, Restaurant Menu

☛ Clyst St Mary stands half a mile from J30 of the M5

🍺 Otter, Bass

🍴 12-2

🎵 Quiz/bingo alternate Sundays; skittle alley/function room

🪑 Beer garden, car park

💳 Major cards accepted

🕐 11-3 & 5-11 (all day Saturday); Sun 12-3 & 7.10.30

🏛 Exeter 1 mile, Exmouth 6 miles

Dating back over 350 years the **Maltsters** is an exquisite inn that enjoys a tranquil village setting yet is only half a mile from the M5. The immaculate black-and-white façade, colourfully adorned in summer, fronts an equally spotless interior, where a recent complete upgrading has enhanced the cosy, appealing ambience. Bubbly Jo Fennell is the driving force here as both host and cook. Sitting on country chairs at sturdy wooden tables, visitors can enjoy an excellent selection of home-cooked dishes, including the all-day breakfast and the Sunday carvery. The pub has a pool table, a skittle alley and a pleasant outside sitting area.

126 The Manor Inn

Lower Ashton, Exeter, Devon EX6 7QL
Tel: 01647 252304

Real Ales, Bar Food, Restaurant Menu,
No Smoking Area, Disabled Facilities

127 **The Mare & Foal**

The Village, Yeoford, Crediton, Devon EX17 5JD
Tel: 01363 84348

Real Ales, Bar Food, Restaurant Menu,
No Smoking Area, Disabled Facilities

See panel below

128 The Marine Tavern

2 Marine Parade, Dawlish, Devon EX7 9DJ
Tel: 01626 865245

Real Ales, Bar Food, Accommodation,
No Smoking Area

---

127 **The Mare & Foal**

Yeoford, nr Crediton, Devon EX17 5JD
☎ 01363 84348 🌐 www.mareandfoal.co.uk

**Real Ales, Bar Food, Restaurant Menu,
No Smoking Area, Disabled Facilities**

- ☛ From Crediton (A39), take minor roads to Yeoford
- 🍺 Doom Bar, Bombardier, Black Sheep
- 🍴 12-2 & 6-9
- ⚒ Garden, car park
- 💳 All the major cards
- 🕐 12-2.30 & 6-11 (all day Sat & Sun)
- 🏛 Crediton 3 miles, Exeter 8 miles

The Mare & Foal was built around 1870 to serve the newly arrived railway, and was originally called the Railway Hotel. New owners Alex and Karen came here from the Bullers Arms at Chagford and bring the same high standards they set there for food, drink and hospitality. All the family are welcome at this substantial inn, where local real ales accompany a fine selection of light meals and hearty classic pub dishes. The inn has a super garden and off-road parking.

129 Market House Inn

21-23 High St, Cullompton, Devon EX15 1AB
Tel: 01884 32339

Disabled Facilities

130 The Merriemeade

1 Lower Town, Sampford Peverell, Tiverton, Devon EX16 7BJ
Tel: 01884 820270

Real Ales, Bar Food, Disabled Facilities

131 The Merry Harriers

Westcott, Cullompton, Devon EX15 1SA
Tel: 01392 881254

Real Ales, Bar Food, Restaurant Menu,
Accommodation, No Smoking Area,
Disabled Facilities

132 Mill End

Chagford, Newton Abbot, Devon TQ13 8JN
Tel: 01647 432282

Bar Food, Restaurant Menu, Accommodation,
No Smoking Area

133 The Mitre

9 High St, Crediton, Devon EX17 3AE
Tel: 01363 772508

Real Ales

134 **The Mitre Inn**

2 The Square, Witheridge, Tiverton,
Devon EX16 8AE
Tel: 01884 861263

Real Ales, Bar Food, Restaurant Menu,
Accommodation, No Smoking Area,
Disabled Facilities

See panel opposite

135 Mount Pleasant Inn

Nomansland, Tiverton, Devon EX16 8NN
Tel: 01884 860271

Real Ales, Bar Food, Restaurant Menu,
No Smoking Area

134 The Mitre Inn

The Square, Witheridge, Devon EX16 8AE

☎ 01884 861263   🌐 www.the-mitre-inn.com

Real Ales, Bar Food, Restaurant Menu, Accommodation, No Smoking Area, Disabled Facilities

- 9 miles W of Tiverton on the B3137
- Exmoor Fox & Wildcat
- 12-2.00 & 6-9.30,
- 4 rooms (2 en suite)
- Quiz Thursday
- Patio, car park
- Major cards accepted
- 12-2.30 (not Mon) & 5-11 (Sun from 6);
- Tiverton 9 miles

The **Mitre** is an imposing stone-built inn in the village of Witheridge. Exmoor Fox is a favourite in the bar, where snacks and meals are served during opening hours. The full food selection is also available lunchtime and evening both in the bar and the non-smoking restaurant, where typical dishes are cod, lasagne and green Thai curry. For staying guests the Mitre has four good-sized bedrooms for B&B.

136 Mount Pleasant Inn

Mount Pleasant Rd, Dawlish Warren, Dawlish, Devon EX7 0NA
Tel: 01626 863151

Real Ales, Bar Food, Restaurant Menu, Accommodation, Disabled Facilities

137 New Fountain Inn

Church Rd, Whimple, Exeter, Devon EX5 2TA
Tel: 01404 822350

Real Ales, Bar Food, Restaurant Menu, No Smoking Area

138 The New Inn

Coleford, Crediton, Devon EX17 5BZ
Tel: 01363 84242

Real Ales, Bar Food, Restaurant Menu, Accommodation, No Smoking Area, Disabled Facilities

139 The New Inn

Sampford Courtenay, Okehampton, Devon EX20 2TB
Tel: 01837 82247

Real Ales, Bar Food, Restaurant Menu, No Smoking Area

See panel on page 100

140 The New Inn

Broadclyst, Exeter, Devon EX5 3BX
Tel: 01392 461312

Real Ales, Bar Food, Restaurant Menu, No Smoking Area, Disabled Facilities

141 Nobody Inn

Doddiscombsleigh, Exeter, Devon EX6 7PS
Tel: 01647 252394

Real Ales, Bar Food, Restaurant Menu, Accommodation

142 Northmore Arms

Throwleigh, Okehampton, Devon EX20 2JA
Tel: 01647 231428

Real Ales, Bar Food, Accommodation

143 The Nutwell Lodge

Exmouth Rd, Lympstone, Exmouth, Devon EX8 5AJ
Tel: 01392 873279

Real Ales, Bar Food, Restaurant Menu, No Smoking Area

144 The Old Coaching House

25 Fore St, Chudleigh, Newton Abbot, Devon TQ13 0HX
Tel: 01626 853270

Real Ales, Bar Food, Restaurant Menu, Accommodation, No Smoking Area

145 The Old Court House

South Molton St, Chulmleigh, Devon EX18 7BW
Tel: 01769 580045

Real Ales, Bar Food, Restaurant Menu, Accommodation, No Smoking Area

See panel on page 100

139 The New Inn

Sampford Courtenay, nr Okehampton,
Devon EX20 2TB

☎ 01837 82247

**Real Ales, Bar Food, Restaurant Menu,
No Smoking Area**

☛ Leave the A30 Exeter-Okehampton road at Whiddon Down on to the A3124 to North Tawton. Left onto A3072 to Samford Courtenay

🍺 Otter and guests

🍴 12-20 & 6-9.20

🛏 Planned to open rooms soon

⛲ Garden, car park

💳 Major cards except Amex and Diners

🕐 11-11 (Sun 12-10.30)

🏛 Okehampton 5 miles, Hatherleigh 5 miles

The New Inn is a distinguished coaching inn with a history that goes back some 500 years. The whitewashed exterior is topped by an immaculate thatched roof, and the inside, sensitively refurbished and updated to retain all the best original features, is warm and welcoming, painted in fetching pastel shades, with heavy ceiling beams (note the inscribed witticisms), open fires and a variety of sofas, tables and chairs. Tenants Anne and Christian Fenton continue the long tradition of hospitality, serving a fine selection of real ales, beers, ciders, lagers, wines, spirits and soft drinks. The food is also excellent, with dishes listed on a large blackboard. The New Inn has a lovely rear garden and an ample off-road car park.

145 The Old Court House

South Molton Street, Chulmleigh,
Devon EX18 7BW

☎ 01769 580045 ☎ www.oldcourthouseinn.co.uk

**Real Ales, Bar Food, Restaurant Menu,
Accommodation, No Smoking Area**

☛ Chulmleigh lies on the B3096 off the A377 Barnstaple-Exeter road

🍺 Bass, Tawny

🍴 11.30-9.30

🛏 Rooms (including 2 en suite) + self-catering

🎵 Quiz Thursday, skittle alley

⛲ Beer garden

💳 Major cards accepted

🕐 11.30-11

🏛 Tarka Trail, 2 Moors Way; South Molton 10 miles

The Coat of Arms on the sign outside the Old Court House bears the date 1633, and it was ten years later that King Charles I stayed here on his first tour of the West Country. Today's visitors will find traditional appeal with up-to-date amenities, and the two en suite bedrooms, including a four-poster room and a family room, provide a very pleasant base for exploring Exmoor, Dartmoor and the other delights of coast and countryside. There's no mistaking the warmth of the greeting from Sam and Paddy Moyse, who provide a day-long choice of real ales, West Country cider, snacks and meals to enjoy in the bar, the non-smoking dining room or out in the cobbled courtyard garden. The pub has a function room and skittle alley. Sam will soon be adding self-catering accommodation to the B&B rooms.

146 The Old Inn
Widecombe-in-the-Moor, Newton Abbot,
Devon TQ13 7TA
Tel: 01364 621207

Real Ales, Bar Food, Restaurant Menu,
No Smoking Area, Disabled Facilities

147 The Old Malt Scoop Inn
Lapford, Crediton, Devon EX17 6PZ
Tel: 01363 83330

Real Ales, Bar Food, Restaurant Menu

148 The Old Thatch Inn
Cheriton Bishop, Exeter, Devon EX6 6JH
Tel: 01647 24204

Real Ales, Bar Food, Restaurant Menu,
Accommodation, No Smoking Area

149 Oxenham Arms Hotel
South Zeal, Okehampton, Devon EX20 2JT
Tel: 01837 840244

Real Ales, Bar Food, Restaurant Menu,
Accommodation, No Smoking Area,
Disabled Facilities

150 Palk Arms Inn
Church Rd Hennock, Newton Abbot,
Devon TQ13 9QB
Tel: 01626 836584

Real Ales, Bar Food, Accommodation,
No Smoking Area

151 Parkway House Hotel
32 Lower Town, Sampford Peverell, Tiverton,
Devon EX16 7BJ
Tel: 01884 820255

Real Ales, Bar Food, Restaurant Menu,
Accommodation, No Smoking Area,
Disabled Facilities

152 The Passage House Inn
Ferry Rd, Topsham, Exeter, Devon EX3 0JN
Tel: 01392 873653

Real Ales, Bar Food, Restaurant Menu,
No Smoking Area

153 The Pilot Inn
5 Chapel Hill, Exmouth, Devon EX8 1NY
Tel: 01395 263382

Real Ales

154 The Poachers Inn
55 High St, Ide, Exeter, Devon EX2 9RW
Tel: 01392 273847

Real Ales, Bar Food, Restaurant Menu,
Accommodation, No Smoking Area

155 The Poltimore Arms
54 Main Rd, Pinhoe, Exeter, Devon EX4 9EY
Tel: 01392 662121

Real Ales, Accommodation, Disabled Facilities

156 Pony & Trap
10 Exeter Hill, Cullompton, Devon EX15 1DJ
Tel: 01884 34968

Disabled Facilities

157 The Post Inn
Exeter Rd, Whiddon Down, Okehampton,
Devon EX20 2QT
Tel: 01647 231242

Real Ales, Bar Food, No Smoking Area

158 The Powder Monkey
2 Parade, Exmouth, Devon EX8 1RJ
Tel: 01395 280090

Real Ales, Bar Food, Restaurant Menu,
No Smoking Area, Disabled Facilities

159 Prince Blucher
98-102 West Exe South, Tiverton,
Devon EX16 5DH
Tel: 01884 232030

Real Ales, Bar Food, Restaurant Menu,
Accommodation, No Smoking Area,
Disabled Facilities
See panel on page 102

160 Prince of Wales
Dinan Way, Exmouth, Devon EX8 4EZ
Tel: 01395 276970

Real Ales, Bar Food, Restaurant Menu

159 The Prince Blucher

West Exe South, Tiverton, Devon EX16 5DH

☎ 01884 232030

**Real Ales, Bar Food, Restaurant Menu,
Accommodation, No Smoking Area,
Disabled Facilities**

- ☞ Close to the centre of Tiverton
- 🍺 Old Speckled hen plus 1 guest ale
- 🍴 12-8, Sun 12-3; all day snacks
- 🛏 6 en suite rooms
- ♫ Live entertainment Friday
- ⚒ Patio
- 💳 Major cards accepted
- ⏰ 11-11 (Sun 12.10.30)
- 🏛 All the attractions of Tiverton are nearby

Apart from Exeter, Tiverton is the only town of any size in the Exe Valley. The Castle, Churches, the School and the Museum are among the many reasons for a visit. Those

in the know add the **Prince Blucher** to their itinerary, and this splendid old inn near the town centre is looking even more splendid after the owning brewery invested a great deal of money in a major improvement programme.

Tenants Tony and Tracy Johnson and their family guarantee a home-from-home experience at this most welcoming of inns, making the bar and lounge delightful spots for enjoying a drink and a chat. Old Speckled Hen is one of the resident real ales, heading a long list of beers, lagers, ciders, wines, spirits and soft drinks. A full and varied menu is available throughout the day in the bar and the full à la carte menu is served in the restaurant from noon to 8 o'clock (Sunday from noon to 3). The sheltered beer garden Is set with tables and chairs under parasols, and patio heaters allow alfresco drinking at most times of the year. Children are welcome inside and outside up to 9 o'clock.

The Prince Blucher is a popular spot for parties, wedding receptions and other special occasions, and the function room can seat up to 50 in comfort. The inn is also a friendly base for both business and leisure visitors, and the six bedrooms offer en suite facilities and up-to-date amenities. The fine buildings are not the only attractions that Tiverton has to offer: a section of the old Great Western Canal provides pleasant walks and a country park, and the gardens at the National Trust's Knightshayes Court, a couple of miles north of town, are among the finest in the county.

161 The Prince Regent

Lowman Green, Tiverton, Devon EX16 4LN

☎ 01884 252882

Real Ales, Accommodation

- ☛ By the familiar landmark of the clock tower in Tiverton, a short drive from the A361 and A396
- 🍺 Prince Regent own brew
- 🛏 5 en suite rooms
- 🎵 Karaoke 3rd Sat of month
- 🅿 Car park
- 🕐 11-11
- 🏛 The sights of Tiverton; Knightshayes NT 2

Prince Regent is the name not only of the pub but of its favourite real ale specially brewed by Courage. Located by the well-known landmark of the clock tower, the pub is very popular with locals, and is also a convenient base for business and leisure visitors with five en suite bedrooms. Pool and darts are played in the bar, and the third Saturday of the moth is karaoke night.

161 The Prince Regent

Lowman Green, Tiverton, Devon EX16 4LA
Tel: 01884 252882

Real Ales, Accommodation

See panel above

162 The Racehorse

Wellbrook St, Tiverton, Devon EX16 5JW
Tel: 01884 252606

Real Ales, Bar Food, Restaurant Menu,
No Smoking Area, Disabled Facilities

163 The Railway Inn

Railway Hotel, North Tawton, Devon EX20 2BE
Tel: 01837 82789

Real Ales, Bar Food, Restaurant Menu

164 The Railway Inn

Beach St, Dawlish, Devon EX7 9PN
Tel: 01626 863226

Real Ales, Bar Food, Accommodation,
No Smoking Area, Disabled Facilities

165 The Red Lion

Shobrooke Village, Crediton, Devon EX17 1AT
Tel: 01363 772340

Real Ales, Bar Food, Restaurant Menu,
Accommodation, No Smoking Area,
Disabled Facilities

See panel below

166 The Red Lion Hotel

East St, Chulmleigh, Devon EX18 7DD
Tel: 01769 580384

Real Ales, Bar Food, Restaurant Menu,
Accommodation

165 The Red Lion Inn

Shobrooke, nr Crediton, Devon EX17 1AT

☎ 01363 772340   🌐 www.theredlioninn.net

**Real Ales, Bar Food, Restaurant Menu,
Accommodation, No Smoking Area,
Disabled Facilities**

- ☛ 2 miles NE of Crediton off the A3072
- 🍺 Sharps, St Austell, O'Hanlons
- 🍴 12-2 & 6.30-9
- 🛏 3 en suite rooms
- 🎵 Quiz Sun
- 🅿 Garden, children's play area, car park
- 💳 Major cards except Amex and Diners
- 🕐 Lunchtime and evening
- 🏛 Crediton 2 miles, Tiverton 9 miles

Guy and Lesley offer a warm welcome at the **Red Lion**, their 16th century inn off the A3072 just outside Crediton. A huge mural of the inn dominates the restaurant, where the excellent home cooking extends over a wide-ranging menu and specials board. Local ales and wines from around the world accompany the fine food, and for guests staying awhile the inn has three en suite bedrooms.

167 The Red Lion Inn
Broadclyst, Exeter, Devon EX5 3EL
Tel: 01392 461271

Real Ales, Bar Food, Restaurant Menu,
Accommodation, No Smoking Area,
Disabled Facilities

168 The Red Lion Inn
Tedburn St. Mary, Exeter, Devon EX6 6EQ
Tel: 01647 61374

Real Ales, Bar Food, Restaurant Menu,
No Smoking Area, Disabled Facilities

169 The Redwing Inn
Church Rd, Lympstone, Exmouth,
Devon EX8 5JT
Tel: 01395 222156

Real Ales, Bar Food, Restaurant Menu,
No Smoking Area, Disabled Facilities

170 Redwoods Inn
Uplowman, Sampford Peverell, Tiverton,
Devon EX16 7DP
Tel: 01884 820148

Real Ales, Bar Food, Restaurant Menu,
No Smoking Area, Disabled Facilities

171 Remedies Bar
9 Gold St, Tiverton, Devon EX16 6QB
Tel: 01884 253347

Real Ales, No Smoking Area, Disabled Facilities

172 Remedies Bar
38-39 The Strand, Exmouth, Devon EX8 1AH
Tel: 01395 224994

Disabled Facilities

173 The Ring O'Bells
44 The Square, Chagford, Newton Abbot,
Devon TQ13 8AH
Tel: 01647 432466

Real Ales, Bar Food, Restaurant Menu,
Accommodation, No Smoking Area

174 The Ring Of Bells
The Hayes, Cheriton Fitzpaine, Crediton,
Devon EX17 4JG
Tel: 01363 866374

Real Ales, Bar Food, Restaurant Menu,
Accommodation, No Smoking Area

175 The Riverbank Hotel
45 Gold St, Tiverton, Devon EX16 6QB
Tel: 01884 254911

Restaurant Menu, Accommodation,
No Smoking Area, Disabled Facilities

176 The Riverside Inn
Fore St, Bovey Tracey, Newton Abbot,
Devon TQ13 9AD
Tel: 01626 832293

Real Ales, Bar Food, Restaurant Menu,
Accommodation, No Smoking Area,
Disabled Facilities

177 Rock Inn
Haytor Vale, Haytor, Newton Abbot,
Devon TQ13 9XP
Tel: 01364 661305

Real Ales, Bar Food, Restaurant Menu,
No Smoking Area

178 Rose & Crown
Sandford, Crediton, Devon EX17 4NH
Tel: 01363 772056

Real Ales, Bar Food, Restaurant Menu,
No Smoking Area

179 Rose & Crown Inn
Calverleigh, Tiverton, Devon EX16 8BA
Tel: 01884 256301

Real Ales, Bar Food, Restaurant Menu,
Accommodation, No Smoking Area,
Disabled Facilities

180 Royal Beacon Hotel
The Beacon, Exmouth, Devon EX8 2AF
Tel: 01395 264886

Bar Food, Restaurant Menu, Accommodation,
No Smoking Area, Disabled Facilities

181 The Royal Oak
Dunsford, Exeter, Devon EX6 7DA
Tel: 01647 252256

Real Ales, Bar Food, Restaurant Menu,
Accommodation, No Smoking Area

182 The Royal Oak
Exminster, Exeter, Devon EX6 8DX
Tel: 01392 832332

Real Ales, Bar Food, No Smoking Area,
Disabled Facilities

183 The Royal Oak Inn
Chawleigh, Chulmleigh, Devon EX18 7HG
Tel: 01769 580427

Real Ales, Bar Food, Restaurant Menu,
Accommodation, No Smoking Area,
Disabled Facilities

184 The Royal Oak Inn
Ideford, Chudleigh, Newton Abbot,
Devon TQ13 0AY
Tel: 01626 852274

Real Ales, Bar Food, Disabled Facilities

185 The Royal Oak
Nadderwater, Exeter, Devon EX4 2JH
Tel: 01392 272352

Real Ales, Bar Food, No Smoking Area

186 The Ruffwell Inn
Thorverton, Exeter, Devon EX5 5NB
Tel: 01392 860377

Real Ales, Restaurant Menu, No Smoking Area,
Disabled Facilities

187 The Rugglestone Inn
Widecombe-in-the-Moor, Newton Abbot,
Devon TQ13 7TF
Tel: 01364 621327

Real Ales, Bar Food, Restaurant Menu,
No Smoking Area, Disabled Facilities

188 The Saddlers Arms
Exmouth Rd, Lympstone, Exmouth,
Devon EX8 5LS
Tel: 01395 272798

Real Ales, Bar Food, Restaurant Menu

189 Salutation Inn
68 Fore St, Topsham, Exeter, Devon EX3 0HL
Tel: 01392 873005

Real Ales, Bar Food, Restaurant Menu,
Accommodation, Disabled Facilities

190 Sampson's Hotel & Restaurant
Preston, Kingsteignton, Newton Abbot,
Devon TQ12 3PP
Tel: 01626 354913

Real Ales, Bar Food, Restaurant Menu,
Accommodation, No Smoking Area,
Disabled Facilities

191 Sandy Park Inn
Sandy Park Chagford, Newton Abbot,
Devon TQ13 8JW
Tel: 01647 433267

Real Ales, Bar Food, Restaurant Menu,
Accommodation, No Smoking Area

192 The Sandygate Inn
Sandygate, Newton Abbot, Devon TQ12 3PU
Tel: 01626 354679

Real Ales, Bar Food

193 Seven Stars
Kennford, Exeter, Devon EX6 7TR
Tel: 01392 833246

Real Ales, Bar Food, Restaurant Menu

194 The Seven Stars
High St, Winkleigh, Devon EX19 8HX
Tel: 01837 83344

Real Ales, Bar Food

195 The Seven Stars Inn
Bridge St, Tiverton, Devon EX16 5LY
Tel: 01884 257272
Disabled Facilities

196 The Seven Stars Inn
South Tawton, Okehampton, Devon EX20 2LW
Tel: 01837 840292
Real Ales, Bar Food, Restaurant Menu,
No Smoking Area

197 Ship Inn
4 Fore St, Chudleigh, Newton Abbot,
Devon TQ13 0HX
Tel: 01626 853268
Real Ales, Bar Food, Disabled Facilities

198 The Ship Inn
High St, Crediton, Devon EX17 3LQ
Tel: 01363 777873

199 The Smugglers Inn
27 Teignmouth Rd, Dawlish, Devon EX7 0LA
Tel: 01626 862301
Real Ales, Bar Food, Restaurant Menu,
No Smoking Area, Disabled Facilities

200 The South Devon Inn
Strand Hill, Dawlish, Devon EX7 9HR
Tel: 01626 862198
Real Ales, Bar Food

201 St George & Dragon
Clyst St. George, Exeter, Devon EX3 0QJ
Tel: 01392 876121
Real Ales, Bar Food, Restaurant Menu,
Accommodation, No Smoking Area,
Disabled Facilities

202 The Star Inn
Liverton, Newton Abbot, Devon TQ12 6EZ
Tel: 01626 821376
Real Ales, Bar Food, Restaurant Menu,
No Smoking Area, Disabled Facilities

203 Steam Packet Inn
1 Monmouth Hill, Topsham, Exeter,
Devon EX3 0JQ
Tel: 01392 875085
Real Ales, Bar Food, Restaurant Menu,
Accommodation, No Smoking Area,
Disabled Facilities

204 Stoke Canon Inn
High St, Stoke Canon, Exeter, Devon EX5 4AR
Tel: 01392 841200
Real Ales, Bar Food, Restaurant Menu,
No Smoking Area, Disabled Facilities

205 The Stowey Arms
Exminster, Exeter, Devon EX6 8AT
Tel: 01392 824216
Real Ales, Bar Food, Restaurant Menu,
No Smoking Area

206 The Strand
1 Parade, Exmouth, Devon EX8 1RS
Tel: 01395 263649
Real Ales, Bar Food, Restaurant Menu,
No Smoking Area, Disabled Facilities

207 Swan Inn
94 Old Town St, Dawlish, Devon EX7 9AT
Tel: 01626 863677
Real Ales, Bar Food, No Smoking Area,
Disabled Facilities

208 The Swan Inn
The Strand, Lympstone, Exmouth,
Devon EX8 5ET
Tel: 01395 270403
Real Ales, Bar Food, Restaurant Menu,
No Smoking Area

209 Teign House Inn
Teign Valley Rd, Christow, Exeter, Devon EX6 7PL
Tel: 01647 252286
Real Ales, Bar Food, No Smoking Area

210 The Teignmouth Inn
Brookdale Cottages, Dawlish, Devon EX7 9PG
Tel: 01626 863037

Real Ales, Bar Food, Accommodation

211 Ten Tors Inn
Exeter Rd, Kingsteignton, Newton Abbot,
Devon TQ12 3NP
Tel: 01626 365434

Real Ales, Bar Food, Restaurant Menu,
No Smoking Area

212 Thelbridge Cross Inn
Thelbridge, Crediton, Devon EX17 4SQ
Tel: 01884 860316

Real Ales, Bar Food, Restaurant Menu,
Accommodation, No Smoking Area,
Disabled Facilities

213 The Thirsty Farmer
Whimple, Exeter, Devon EX5 2QQ
Tel: 01404 822287

Real Ales, Restaurant Menu, No Smoking Area

214 Thorverton Arms
The Berry, Thorverton, Exeter, Devon EX5 5NS
Tel: 01392 860205

Real Ales, Bar Food, Restaurant Menu,
Accommodation, No Smoking Area,
Disabled Facilities

215 Three Crowns
High St, Chagford, Newton Abbot,
Devon TQ13 8AJ
Tel: 01647 433444

Real Ales, Bar Food, Restaurant Menu,
Accommodation, No Smoking Area,
Disabled Facilities

216 The Three Little Pigs
Parliament St, Crediton, Devon EX17 2BP
Tel: 01363 774587

Real Ales, Bar Food, Restaurant Menu,
No Smoking Area

217 The Three Tuns Inn
14 Exeter Rd, Silverton, Exeter, Devon EX5 4HX
Tel: 01392 860352

Real Ales, Bar Food, Restaurant Menu,
Accommodation, No Smoking Area,
Disabled Facilities

218 The Tom Cobley Tavern
Spreyton, Devon EX17 5AL
Tel: 01647 231314

Real Ales, Bar Food, Restaurant Menu,
Accommodation, No Smoking Area,
Disabled Facilities

219 Travellers Rest
Tedburn Rd, Whitestone, Exeter,
Devon EX4 2HQ
Tel: 01392 811217

Real Ales, Bar Food, Restaurant Menu,
No Smoking Area, Disabled Facilities

220 The Trout Inn
Bickleigh, Tiverton, Devon EX16 8RJ
Tel: 01884 855596

Real Ales, Bar Food, Restaurant Menu,
No Smoking Area, Disabled Facilities

221 Turf Hotel
Exminster, Exeter, Devon EX6 8EE
Tel: 01392 833128

Real Ales, Bar Food, Restaurant Menu,
No Smoking Area, Disabled Facilities

222 The Twisted Oak
Ide, Exeter, Devon EX2 9RG
Tel: 01392 273666

Real Ales, Bar Food, Restaurant Menu,
No Smoking Area, Disabled Facilities

223 The Twyford Inn
Bampton St, Tiverton, Devon EX16 6AL
Tel: 01884 252019

Real Ales, Bar Food, Restaurant Menu,
No Smoking Area, Disabled Facilities

224 The Union Inn

10 Ford St, Moretonhampstead, Newton Abbot,
Devon TQ13 8LN
Tel: 01647 440199

Real Ales, Bar Food, Restaurant Menu

225 The Waie Inn

Zeal Monachorum, Crediton, Devon EX17 6DF
Tel: 01363 82348

Real Ales, Bar Food, Restaurant Menu,
Accommodation, No Smoking Area,
Disabled Facilities

226 The Warren House Inn

Postbridge, Yelverton, Devon PL20 6TA
Tel: 01822 880208

Real Ales, Bar Food, Restaurant Menu,
No Smoking Area, Disabled Facilities

227 The Weary Traveller

Station Rd, Cullompton, Devon EX15 1BQ
Tel: 01884 32317

Real Ales, Bar Food, Restaurant Menu,
No Smoking Area, Disabled Facilities

228 Welcome Inn

Dawlish Warren, Dawlish, Devon EX7 0NE
Tel: 01626 888577

Real Ales, Bar Food, Restaurant Menu,
No Smoking Area

229 White Ball Inn

8 Bridge St, Tiverton, Devon EX16 5LY
Tel: 01884 251525

Real Ales, Bar Food, Restaurant Menu,
No Smoking Area, Disabled Facilities

232 The White Hart

Fore Street, Cullompton, Devon EX15 1JS
☎ 01884 33260

**Real Ales, Bar Food, Restaurant Menu,
Accommodation**

☛ On the main street of Cullompton, B3181 5
miles SE of Tiverton

🍺 Courage

🍴 12-2.30 & 6-9.30 (no food Sunday)

🛏 3 en suite rooms

🕐 11-Midnight (Sun 12-23.30)

🏛 Cullompton's Church of St Andrew; Tiverton 5
miles, Exeter 10 miles

Five miles from Tiverton and just minutes
from J28 of the M5, the **White Hart** is a
very pleasant spot to pause for refreshment or
to enjoy a meal.

Dating from the 16th century, this attractive
listed building on the main street of
Cullompton also provides a friendly base for
both business and leisure visitors, and the
three guest bedrooms all have en suite
facilities.

Food is served every lunchtime and evening
Monday to Saturday, and the big blackboard
menu offers everything from sandwiches,
ploughman's platters and jacket potatoes to
meat, fish and vegetarian main courses. Pool,
darts and skittles are the favourite pub games.

230 The White Hart
6 Albert St, Dawlish, Devon EX7 9JY
Tel: 01626 866476

Real Ales

231 White Hart
58 Fore St, North Tawton, Devon EX20 2DT
Tel: 01837 82473

Real Ales, Bar Food, Restaurant Menu,
No Smoking Area, Disabled Facilities

232 **White Hart Inn**
19 Fore St, Cullompton, Devon EX15 1JS
Tel: 01884 33260

Real Ales, Bar Food, Restaurant Menu,
Accommodation

See panel opposite

233 White Hart Inn
Church St, Woodbury, Exeter, Devon EX5 1HN
Tel: 01395 232221

Real Ales, Bar Food, Restaurant Menu,
No Smoking Area, Disabled Facilities

234 White Horse Inn
12 Gold St, Tiverton, Devon EX16 6PZ
Tel: 01884 252022

Real Ales, Accommodation, Disabled Facilities

235 White Horse Inn
White Horse Inn, Woodbury Salterton, Exeter,
Devon EX5 1EP
Tel: 01395 232244

Real Ales, Bar Food, Restaurant Menu,
No Smoking Area

236 White Horse Inn
7 The Square, Moretonhampstead,
Newton Abbot, Devon TQ13 8NF
Tel: 01647 440242

Real Ales

237 White Lion Inn
26 High St, Bradninch, Exeter, Devon EX5 4QL
Tel: 01392 881263

Real Ales, Bar Food, Restaurant Menu,
Accommodation

238 The White Swan
33 High St, Crediton, Devon EX17 3JP
Tel: 01363 772694

Real Ales

239 York Inn
21 Imperial Rd, Exmouth, Devon EX8 1BY
Tel: 01395 222488

Real Ales, Bar Food, Disabled Facilities

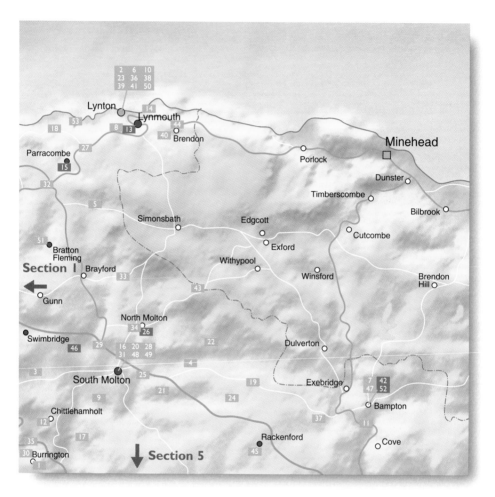

2 6 10
23 36 38
39 41 50

Lynton

14
Lynmouth

18 53

8 13

44
40 Brendon

27

Parracombe

15

Minehead

Porlock

Dunster

32

5

Timberscombe

Bilbrook

Simonsbath

Edgcott

Cutcombe

51

Bratton
Fleming

Exford

Section 1 Brayford

Withypool

33

43

Winsford

Brendon
Hill

Gunn

North Molton

34 26

Dulverton

Swimbridge

46

29

16 20 28
31 48 49

22

3

25

South Molton

21

19

24

Exebridge

7 42
47 52

9

Bampton

Chittlehamholt

37

12

17

11

35

Rackenford

Cove

30 Burrington

45

1

↓ Section 5

■ 11 ■ Pub or Inn Reference Number - Detailed Information

12 Pub or Inn Reference Number - Summary Entry

● ■ Place of interest mentioned in the chapter introduction

NORTH DEVON COAST (EAST) AND EXMOOR

The chief communities of this stretch of coast are Lynmouth at sea level and Lynton on the cliff above, the two linked by a unique water-powered railway. Inland lies Exmoor, much less bleak than Dartmoor, Devon's other National Park.

Bratton Fleming

Attractions close to this village include **Exmoor Zoological Park**, the nature reserve at **Wistlandpound Reservoir** and the National Trust's **Arlington Court**, home from 1534 to 1949 of the Chichester family. The round-the-world yachtsman Sir Francis Chichester, the best-known member of the family, was born just 2 miles away at Shirwell and is buried there in the churchyard of **St Peter's**.

Lynmouth

Lynmouth made worldwide news in 1952 when the East Lyn river burst its banks and flooded the village. The **Flood Memorial Hall** recounts the events in a poignant exhibition. In the **Exmoor Brass Rubbing and Hobbycraft Centre**, visitors can have a go at taking a rubbing from

one of the more than 2,000 facsimiles of brasses dating back as far as 1277. Lynmouth on the shore and **Lynton** on a great cliff above are linked by the extraordinary water-powered **Cliff Railway**, which covers a vertical height of 500 feet at a gradient of 1 in 1.175. The **Lyn and Exmoor Museum** traces the history of the twin towns and of Exmoor National Park. To the west of Lynton lies the famous **Valley of the Rocks**.

Lynmouth

Parracombe

The redundant **Church of St Petrock**, is notable for its marvellously unspoilt interior. Perhaps the most striking feature is the unique gated screen between the chancel and the nave that bears a huge tympanum painted with the Royal Arms, the Lord's Prayer, the Creed and the Ten Commandments. The survival of this church is due to John Ruskin, who led protests against its proposed demolition in 1879 after another church was built lower down the hill.

Valley of the Rocks, Lynton

Rackenford

The **Rackenford and Knowstone Moors Nature Reserve** encompasses a unique habitat of wet grassland, heath, bog and scrub. It supports a wealth of wildlife and in particular is a haven for butterflies.

South Molton

In and around Broad Street stand many of the town's most distinguished buildings, including the **Market Hall**, the **Assembly Rooms**, the **Guildhall** and the old **Medical hall** with its iron balcony and four Ionic columns. On the outskirts lies **Quince Honey Farm** with the world's biggest living honeybee exhibition.

Swimbridge

The best-known resident of Swimbridge was the Rev John Russell, the hunting parson who bred the first Jack Russell terriers. This colourful character, who died in 1880, is buried in the churchyard of **St James**. Just outside Swimbridge is the **North Devon Farm Park**, centred round a traditional 15th century Devon farmhouse and offering an insight into old farming methods as well as a host of family attractions.

1 The Barnstaple Inn

Barnstaple Inn Cottage, Burrington, Umberleigh,
Devon EX37 9JG
Tel: 01769 520457

Real Ales

2 Bath Hotel

Lynmouth St, Lynmouth, Devon EX35 6EL
Tel: 01598 752238

Real Ales, Bar Food, Restaurant Menu,
Accommodation, No Smoking Area,
Disabled Facilities

3 The Bell

Chittlehampton, Umberleigh, Devon EX37 9QL
Tel: 01769 540368

Real Ales, Bar Food, No Smoking Area,
Disabled Facilities

4 The Black Cock

Molland, South Molton, Devon EX36 3NW
Tel: 01769 550297

Real Ales, Bar Food, Restaurant Menu,
Accommodation, No Smoking Area

5 Black Venus Inn

Challacombe, Nr Barnstaple, Devon EX31 4TT
Tel: 01598 763251

Real Ales, Bar Food, Restaurant Menu,
No Smoking Area

6 Bonnicott House Hotel

10 Watersmeet Rd, Lynmouth, Devon EX35 6EP
Tel: 01598 753346

Restaurant Menu, Accommodation,
No Smoking Area

7 Bridge House

24 Luke St, Bampton, Tiverton,
Devon EX16 9NF
Tel: 01398 331298

Real Ales, Bar Food, Restaurant Menu,
No Smoking Area

8 Bridge Inn

Lynbridge, Lynton, Devon EX35 6NR
Tel: 01598 753425

Real Ales, Bar Food, Restaurant Menu,
Accommodation, No Smoking Area

9 Castle Inn

George Nympton, South Molton,
Devon EX36 4JE
Tel: 01769 572633

Real Ales, Bar Food, Restaurant Menu,
Accommodation, No Smoking Area

10 The Crown Hotel

Market St, Lynton, Devon EX35 6AG
Tel: 01598 752253

Real Ales, Bar Food, Restaurant Menu,
Accommodation, No Smoking Area

11 Exeter Inn

Bampton, Tiverton, Devon EX16 9DY
Tel: 01398 331345

Real Ales, Bar Food, Restaurant Menu,
Accommodation, No Smoking Area,
Disabled Facilities

12 Exeter Inn

Chittlehamholt, Umberleigh, Devon EX37 9NS
Tel: 01769 540281

Real Ales, Bar Food, Restaurant Menu,
Accommodation, No Smoking Area

13 Exmoor Manor Hotel & Beggars Roost

Barbrook, Lynton, Devon EX35 6LD
Tel: 01598 752404

Real Ales, Bar Food, Restaurant Menu,
Accommodation, No Smoking Area,
Disabled Facilities

See panel on page 114

14 Exmoor Sandpiper Inn

Countisbury, Lynton, Devon EX35 6NE
Tel: 01598 741263

Real Ales, Bar Food, Restaurant Menu,
Accommodation, No Smoking Area,
Disabled Facilities

13 Exmoor Manor Hotel & Beggars Roost Restaurant

Barbrook, nr Lynton, Devon EX35 6LD

☎ 01598 752404   🌐 www.exmoormanorhotel.co.uk

Real Ales, Bar Food, Restaurant Menu, Accommodation, No Smoking Area, Disabled Facilities

- On the A39 on the Lynton/Lynmouth side of Barbrook
- Exmoor Classic + guests
- 12-2.30 & 6-9
- 7 en suite rooms
- Regular live music and theme nights
- Gardens, patio, car park
- All the major cards
- 12-3 & 6-11
- Lynton & Lynmouth 3 miles, Valley of the Rocks 3 miles

Visitors to the **Exmoor Manor Hotel** will find all the best attributes of a country hotel, a fine restaurant and a cheerful village pub. Easily found on the A39, this friendly, well-run place makes an ideal base for a relaxing break exploring the surrounding countryside and the North Devon coast. The hotel has seven en suite rooms, including two family rooms and two four-posters. The tariff includes a full English breakfast, and evening meals can be enjoyed in the adjoining Beggars Roost Restaurant. This convivial pub serves real ales and other beers and a good choice of wines to complement the excellent home-cooked food (hand-made pork pie, cheese & ham quiche, potted crab, steak & kidney casserole with dumplings). The hotel and inn share a large lawned garden.

15 Fox & Goose

Parracombe, Barnstaple, Devon EX31 4PE
Tel: 01598 763239

Real Ales, Bar Food, Accommodation, No Smoking Area, Disabled Facilities

See panel opposite

16 The George Hotel

Broad St, South Molton, Devon EX36 3AB
Tel: 01769 572514

Real Ales, Bar Food, Restaurant Menu, Accommodation, No Smoking Area, Disabled Facilities

17 The Grove Inn

Kings Nympton, Umberleigh, Devon EX37 9ST
Tel: 01769 580406

Real Ales, Bar Food, Restaurant Menu, No Smoking Area, Disabled Facilities

18 The Hunters Inn

Heddon Valley, Parracombe, Barnstaple, Devon EX31 4PY
Tel: 01598 763230

Real Ales, Bar Food, Restaurant Menu, Accommodation, No Smoking Area, Disabled Facilities

19 The Jubilee Inn

West Anstey, South Molton, Devon EX36 3PH
Tel: 01398 341401

Real Ales, Bar Food, Restaurant Menu, No Smoking Area, Disabled Facilities

20 Kings Arms

4 King St, South Molton, Devon EX36 3BL
Tel: 01769 572679

Real Ales, Disabled Facilities

15 The Fox & Goose

Parracombe, nr Barnstaple, Devon EX31 4PE
☎ 01598 763239

**Real Ales, Bar Food, Accommodation,
No Smoking Area, Disabled Facilities**

☛ Parracombe is located off the A39 5 miles SW of Lynmouth

🍺 Barn Owl, Silver Stallion, Dartmoor Best

🍴 12-2 & 6-9

🛏 1 double room en suite

🚗 Beer garden, car park

💳 All the major cards

🕐 12-11

🏛 Church of St Petroc; Lynmouth 5 miles

A log fire, wooden ceiling, antlers and horns, sturdy furniture and old photographs give a real Moorland feel to the Fox & Goose, which enjoys a quiet setting in a village off the A39. The inn has earned a fine reputation for the quality of its cooking, and hosts Paul and Nikki attract visitors from near and far with a regularly daily changing menu based on the very best local produce. The blackboard offers a tempting choice of fish, meat and game dishes, and for those who can't decide between the two the popular surf 'n' turf solves the problem. The food is complemented by plenty of wines by glass or bottle, and West Country ales and farmhouse cider. The inn has a double en suite room for guests exploring the delights of the area.

21 Kings Crow

Bishops Nympton, South Molton,
Devon EX36 4PQ
Tel: 01769 550697

Real Ales, Bar Food, Restaurant Menu,
No Smoking Area, Disabled Facilities

22 The London Inn

Molland, South Molton, Devon EX36 3NG
Tel: 01769 550269

Real Ales, Bar Food, Restaurant Menu,
Accommodation, No Smoking Area,
Disabled Facilities

23 Lynton Cottage Hotel

North Walk, Lynton, Devon EX35 6ED
Tel: 01598 752342

Bar Food, Restaurant Menu, Accommodation,
No Smoking Area, Disabled Facilities

24 The Masons Arms

Knowstone, South Molton, Devon EX36 4RY
Tel: 01398 341231

Real Ales, Restaurant Menu, No Smoking Area

25 Mill Inn

Bishmill, South Molton, Devon EX36 3QF
Tel: 01769 550944

Real Ales, Bar Food, Restaurant Menu,
No Smoking Area, Disabled Facilities

26 The Miners Arms

East St, North Molton, South Molton,
Devon EX36 3HT
Tel: 01598 740316

Real Ales, Bar Food, Restaurant Menu,
No Smoking Area, Disabled Facilities

See panel on page 116

26 The Miners Arms

East Street, North Molton, Devon EX36 3HT

☎ 01598 740316

**Real Ales, Bar Food, Restaurant Menu,
No Smoking Area, Disabled Facilities**

☞ North Molton lies off the A361 3 miles N of
South Molton

🍺 Exmoor Fox

🍴 12-2 & 6-9

🎵 Skittles (3 pub teams), pool, darts

⛺ Garden, car park

🕐 12-11

🏛 Parish church and Court Barton in North
Molton, Exmoor National Park 1 mile, South
Molton 3 miles

The town of North Molton was once a centre of mining, a heritage remembered in the name of the **Miners Arms**. Ales from local breweries are on tap in the bar, where a huge open fire keeps things cosy. Food is served every session in the restaurant.

27 Moorlands

Woody Bay, Parracombe, Barnstaple,
Devon EX31 4RA
Tel: 01598 763224

Restaurant Menu, Accommodation

28 New Inn

28-29 South St, South Molton,
Devon EX36 4AE
Tel: 01769 572546

Real Ales, No Smoking Area

29 The North Gate Inn

Aller Cross Roundabout, South Molton,
Devon EX36 3RG
Tel: 01769 579555

Real Ales, Bar Food, Restaurant Menu

30 Northcote Manor Hotel

Burrington, Umberleigh, Devon EX37 9LZ
Tel: 01769 560501

Bar Food, Restaurant Menu, Accommodation,
No Smoking Area, Disabled Facilities

31 The Old Coaching Inn

Queen St, South Molton, Devon EX36 3BJ
Tel: 01769 572526

Real Ales, Bar Food

32 The Old Station House Inn

Blackmore Gate, Kentisbury, Barnstaple,
Devon EX31 4NW
Tel: 01598 763520

Real Ales, Bar Food, Restaurant Menu,
No Smoking Area

33 Poltimore Arms

Yarde Down, South Molton, Devon EX36 3HA
Tel: 01598 710381

Real Ales, Bar Food, Restaurant Menu,
No Smoking Area

34 Poltimore Inn

East St, North Molton, South Molton,
Devon EX36 3HR
Tel: 01598 740338

Real Ales, Bar Food, Restaurant Menu,
No Smoking Area, Disabled Facilities

35 Portsmouth Arms Hotel

Burrington, Umberleigh, Devon EX37 9ND
Tel: 01769 560397

Real Ales, Bar Food, Restaurant Menu,
Accommodation, No Smoking Area,
Disabled Facilities

36 Queens Hotel
8 Queen St, Lynton, Devon EX35 6AA
Tel: 01598 753388

Real Ales, Bar Food, No Smoking Area

37 The Red Lion
Rookery Hill, Oakford, Tiverton,
Devon EX16 9ES
Tel: 01398 351219

Real Ales, Bar Food, Restaurant Menu,
Accommodation, No Smoking Area,
Disabled Facilities

38 Rising Sun Hotel
Harbourside, Lynmouth, Devon EX35 6EG
Tel: 01598 753223

Real Ales, Bar Food, Restaurant Menu,
Accommodation, No Smoking Area

39 The Rock House Hotel
Rock House, Lynmouth, Devon EX35 6EN
Tel: 01598 753508

Real Ales, Bar Food, Restaurant Menu,
Accommodation, No Smoking Area,
Disabled Facilities

40 The Rockford Inn
Brendon, Lynton, Devon EX35 6PT
Tel: 01598 741214

Real Ales, Bar Food, Restaurant Menu,
Accommodation, No Smoking Area,
Disabled Facilities

41 The Sandrock Hotel
Longmead, Lynton, Devon EX35 6DH
Tel: 01598 753307

Real Ales, Bar Food, Restaurant Menu,
Accommodation, No Smoking Area

42 The Seahorse Inn
Briton St, Bampton, Tiverton, Devon EX16 9LN
Tel: 01398 331480

Real Ales, Bar Food, Restaurant Menu,
Accommodation, No Smoking Area,
Disabled Facilities

See panel adjacent

42 The Seahorse Inn
Briton Street, Bampton, Devon EX16 9LN
☎ 01398 331480

**Real Ales, Bar Food, Restaurant Menu,
Accommodation, No Smoking Area,
Disabled Facilities**

- 🖝 Off the A361 5 miles N of Tiverton
- 🍺 Bombardier
- 🍴 12-2 & 7-9; all day snacks
- 🛏 3 en suite rooms
- 🎵 Live music every other Sun, karaoke first Fri of month
- 🅿 Car park
- 💳 All the major cards
- 🕐 12-3 & 6-11 (all day Sat & Sun)
- 🏛 Exmoor 4 miles, Tiverton 5 miles

The **Seahorse** began life as a staging inn on the Exeter-Minehead coaching route. The long tradition of hospitality is maintained in style by Eileeen, Rob and Lynn, and the bar is a cheerful spot to enjoy lively conversation and a glass of ale. A good choice of dishes is served lunchtime and evening, and meals finish with home-made puddings. There are 3 en suite rooms.

43 The Sportmans Inn
Sandyway, South Molton, Devon EX36 3LU
Tel: 01643 831109

Real Ales, Bar Food, Restaurant Menu,
No Smoking Area, Disabled Facilities

44 The Stag Hunters Hotel
Brendon, Lynton, Devon EX35 6PS
Tel: 01598 741222

Real Ales, Bar Food, Restaurant Menu,
Accommodation, No Smoking Area,
Disabled Facilities

45 The Stag Inn
Rackenford, Tiverton, Devon EX16 8DT
Tel: 01884 881369

Real Ales, Bar Food, No Smoking Area

46 The Stags Head Inn

Filleigh, nr Barnstaple, Devon EX32 0RN

☎ 01598 760250 ⊞ www.stagshead.co.uk

Real Ales, Bar Food, Restaurant Menu, Accommodation, No Smoking Area, Disabled Facilities

- ☛ Leave A361 west of South Molton, southeast of Barnstaple on to B3226, following signs to Filleigh
- 🍺 Bass, Greene King IPA
- 🍴 12-2 & 7-9
- 🛏 4 rooms
- ⚓ Terrace garden by pond, car park
- 💳 All the major cards
- 🕐 12-2.30 & 6-11
- 🏛 Castle Hill Gardens; South Molton 4 miles, Barnstaple 6 miles

Nestling in its own secluded valley near the beautiful Castle Hill Estate, the **Stags Head** is a charming thatched and flagstoned Inn dating back to the 16th century. The gardens at Castle Hill are a sheer delight and just one of the many reasons to tarry hereabouts, and the Inn has four comfortable B&B rooms in a wing with its own entrance. Proprietors Sue, Sally and John and their team welcome young and old alike to their Inn, which deserves its reputation as both a friendly local and one of the best eating places in the region. The menu includes everything from bar snacks and meals to an evening à la carte that showcases Sue's talents with an impressive array of fish, meat and vegetarian dishes representing the very best of British cuisine.

52 The White Horse

Fore Street, Bampton, Devon EX16 9ND

☎ 01398 331245

Real Ales, Bar Food, Restaurant Menu, Accommodation, No Smoking Area

- ☛ Off the A361 5 miles N of Tiverton
- 🍺 John Smith, Old Speckled Hen
- 🍴 12-2.30 & 6-9 (all day Sat & Sun); quick snacks all day
- 🛏 7 en suite rooms
- 🎵 Jam session Monday, live music Fri & Sat
- ⚓ Patio
- 💳 Major cards accepted
- 🕐 12-3 & 5-11 (all day Fri-Sun)
- 🏛 Exmoor 4 miles, Tiverton 5 miles

Bampton is known far and wide for its annual Exmoor Pony Sale in October, but the **White Horse** is an attraction throughout the year. Martyn and Pauline Upton have recently taken the reins at this charming 17th century village inn, where they welcome young and old, locals and new faces into the cheerful surroundings of the bar. A selection of well-kept real ales is always on tap, and freshly prepared, unpretentious pub dishes offer excellent value for money. Seven en suite bedrooms provide a comfortable base for a quiet break or a touring holiday, with Exmoor and the coast to the north and the lovely old wool town of Tiverton a short drive to the south.

46 Stags Head Inn

Filleigh, Barnstaple, Devon EX32 0RN
Tel: 01598 760250

Real Ales, Bar Food, Restaurant Menu,
Accommodation, No Smoking Area,
Disabled Facilities

See panel opposite

47 The Swan Hotel

Station Rd, Bampton, Tiverton,
Devon EX16 9NG
Tel: 01398 331257

Real Ales, Bar Food, Restaurant Menu,
Accommodation, No Smoking Area,
Disabled Facilities

48 Tiverton Inn

18 East St, South Molton, Devon EX36 3DB
Tel: 01769 572525

Real Ales, Bar Food, Restaurant Menu,
Accommodation, No Smoking Area,
Disabled Facilities

49 The Town Arms Hotel

East St, South Molton, Devon EX36 3BU
Tel: 01769 572531

Real Ales, Bar Food, Accommodation,
No Smoking Area

50 The Village Inn

Lynmouth St, Lynmouth, Devon EX35 6EH
Tel: 01598 752354

Real Ales, Bar Food, Restaurant Menu,
Accommodation, No Smoking Area,
Disabled Facilities

51 White Hart

Bratton Fleming, Barnstaple, Devon EX31 4SA
Tel: 01598 710977

Real Ales, Bar Food, Restaurant Menu,
No Smoking Area, Disabled Facilities

52 White Horse Inn

Fore St, Bampton, Tiverton, Devon EX16 9ND
Tel: 01398 331245

Real Ales, Bar Food, Restaurant Menu,
Accommodation, No Smoking Area

See panel opposite

53 Woody Bay

Woody Bay, Parracombe, Barnstaple,
Devon EX31 4QX
Tel: 01598 763264

Bar Food, Restaurant Menu, Accommodation,
No Smoking Area

Section 5

Section 7

11 Pub or Inn Reference Number - Detailed Information

12 Pub or Inn Reference Number - Summary Entry

● ■ Place of interest mentioned in the chapter introduction

EAST DEVON AND THE HERITAGE COAST

Sidmouth and Seaton are the main areas of population on the Heritage Coast, while inland lie Honiton, a renowned centre of lace-making, and Axminster, famed for its luxurious woven carpets. Beer also has a long tradition of lace-making, while historical interest runs from Iron Age forts to a museum remembering British and American pilots in the Second World War.

Axminster

Axminster was an important religious centre in the Middle Ages but is best known for its carpets, made here since 1755. Carpets are still made in Axminster, and visitors can watch the process in the factory. The town's old police station and courthouse is home to the fascinating **town museum**.

Beer

This picturesque fishing village has a long history of lacemaking, and in 1899 Beer lacemakers produced the trimmings for Queen Victoria's wedding dress. Quarrying was also an important industry, and visitors can take a

guided tour of the underground caverns at **Beer Quarry Caves**.

Branscombe

A scattered village of farmhouses and cottages on one of the most spectacular stretches of the Heritage Coast in East Devon. Branscombe is home to the what was the last traditional working bakery in Devon; now in the care of the National

Beach at Beer

Branscombe Church

home to **Burrow Farm Gardens**, 10 acres of beautifully landscaped gardens that include a pergola walk and the Millennium Rill Garden.

Dunkeswell

The 900-year-old font in the **Church of Saint Nicholas** has the earliest known representation of an elephant in England. The font came originally from **Dunkeswell Abbey**, of which only the gatehouse remains. To the west of the village lies **Dunkeswell Memorial Museum**, a memorial to American and British personnel who served at the base, the only American Navy Air Base commissioned on British soil during World War II.

Honiton

This delightful little town in the Otter Valley was the first in Devon to manufacture serge cloth, but has become much better known for its lace. **Allhallows Museum** is one of the few buildings that survived a series of fires in the mid-18th century, and another is **Marwood House**, built in 1619 for one of Elizabeth I's physicians.

Musbury

The village is overlooked by **Musbury Castle**, an Iron Age earthwork hill fort. The village church contains the renowned Drake Memorial from 1611.

Trust, the **Old Bakery** is supplied with flour from the adjacent water-powered mill.

Budleigh Salterton

With its neat Victorian villas, broad promenade and beach flanked by red sandstone cliffs, Budleigh Salterton retains its genteel 19th century resort atmosphere. One famous Victorian visitor was the artist Millais, who painted his most famous work *The Boyhood of Raleigh* beside the beach. The **Otter Estuary Nature Reserve** covers the whole of the estuary.

Colyford

Throughout its long history, Colyton has been an important agricultural and commercial centre, with its corn mill, tannery, saw mill and iron foundry. It lies at one end of the **Seaton Tramway**.

Dalwood

Loughwood Meeting House is one of the oldest surviving Baptist chapels in the country, built in the 1650s. Dalwood is also

Otterton

The Domesday Book recorded a mill here on the banks of the River Otter, on a site almost certainly occupied by the present **Otterton Mill**. This handsome part-medieval building still produces flour, and the Mill Museum tells the story of the mill and its workings.

Ottery St Mary

The glory of the town is its magnificent 14th century **Church of St Mary**, modelled on Exeter Cathedral. Its treasures include a brilliantly coloured alter screen, canopied tombs and a 14th century astronomical clock. A bronze plaque commemorates Samuel Taylor Coleridge, the town's most famous son. A mile outside the town stands historic **Cadhay Manor**, a 16th century manor house approached by an avenue of limes.

Seaton

At the mouth of the River Axe, this pleasant seaside town boasts many handsome Victorian buildings, well-kept public parks, a walled promenade, a pretty harbour and a vast pebbled beach. The **Seaton Tramway** provides a particularly attractive means of travelling along the Axe Valley through two nature reserves up to Colyton, 3 miles inland.

Shute

Shute Barton (NT) is an exceptional example of a non-fortified medieval manor house; among the many impressive features are the Great Hall, the Great Kitchen (with an open fireplace believed to be the largest in the country) and a Tudor gatehouse.

Sidbury

Notable features in the **Church of St Peter and St Giles** include a room where gunpowder was stored, a Saxon crypt and a 500-year-old font. Sidbury is also home to **Sidbury Hill Art Gallery**, while above the village stands the Iron Age hill fort of **Sidbury Castle**. Also nearby is one of Devon's hidden gems – the mainly Elizabethan **Sand House and Gardens**.

Sidmouth

A walk round this elegant resort reveals a wealth of fine buildings (nearly 500 listed). Close to the seafront is the **Sid Vale Heritage Centre**, which tells the story of the town through old photographs, costumes and Victoriana. Just outside the town, on the road to Lyme Regis, is the **Donkey Sanctuary**, home to some 400 rescued donkeys. Neighbouring **Sidford** is famous for its Norman **Packhorse Bridge**.

1   The Anchor

Fore St, Beer, Seaton, Devon EX12 3ET
Tel: 01297 20386

Real Ales, Bar Food, Restaurant Menu,
Accommodation, No Smoking Area

2   The Anchor Inn

Old Fore St, Sidmouth, Devon EX10 8LP
Tel: 01395 514129

Real Ales, Bar Food, No Smoking Area,
Disabled Facilities

See panel below

3   Awliscombe Inn

Awliscombe, Honiton, Devon EX14 3PJ
Tel: 01404 42554

Real Ales, Restaurant Menu, Accommodation,
No Smoking Area, Disabled Facilities

4   Axminster Inn

Silver St, Axminster, Devon EX13 5AH
Tel: 01297 34947

Real Ales

5   Ayshford Arms

Station Rd, Burlescombe, Tiverton,
Devon EX16 7JN
Tel: 01823 672418

Real Ales

6   The Balfour Arms

26 Woolbrook Rd, Sidmouth, Devon EX10 9UZ
Tel: 01395 512993

Real Ales, Bar Food, Restaurant Menu,
No Smoking Area, Disabled Facilities

7   Barrel of Beer

Fore St, Beer, Seaton, Devon EX12 3EQ
Tel: 01297 20099

Real Ales, Bar Food, Restaurant Menu,
No Smoking Area

8   The Bedford Hotel

The Esplanade, Sidmouth, Devon EX10 8NR
Tel: 01395 513047

Real Ales, Bar Food, Restaurant Menu,
Accommodation, No Smoking Area

---

2   The Anchor Inn

Old Fore Street, Sidmouth, Devon EX10 8LP
☎ 01395 514129

**Real Ales, Bar Food, No Smoking Area,
Disabled Facilities**

- In the town centre close to the sea
- One changing
- 12-8 (Sun 12-3)
- Patio, car park
- Major cards accepted
- 11-11
- Seafront short walk, Sidford 1½ miles, Sidbury 2½ miles, Branscombe Manor NT 4 miles, Otterton Mill 3 miles

Trevor, Denise, Matthew and Michelle make a fine family team at the Anchor Inn, which enjoys a prime location in the town centre, a short stroll from the seafront. The large floor space in the smartly revamped bar allows plenty of space for tables and chairs, and a few more are set out at the front for fine-weather sipping; at the back is a much larger area set with picnic benches. The hosts regularly rotate the cask ales and offer a full range of other beers and lagers. Food is an important element in the inn's popularity, and many regulars drop anchor here to enjoy an extensive menu served from noon to 8 o'clock Monday to Saturday and from noon to 3 o'clock on Sunday. Favourite dishes include fresh fish specials, gammon, steak & ale pie, pizza and pasta.

9 The Belmont

The Esplanade, Sidmouth, Devon EX10 8RX
Tel: 01395 512555

Bar Food, Restaurant Menu, Accommodation,
No Smoking Area, Disabled Facilities

10 Black Horse Inn

Fore St, Sidmouth, Devon EX10 8AQ
Tel: 01395 513676

Real Ales, Bar Food, Restaurant Menu,
No Smoking Area, Disabled Facilities

11 The Blacksmiths Arms

Plymtree, Cullompton, Devon EX15 2JU
Tel: 01884 277474

Real Ales, Bar Food, Restaurant Menu,
No Smoking Area

12 The Blue Ball Inn

Stevens Cross, Sidford, Sidmouth,
Devon EX10 9QL
Tel: 01395 514062

Real Ales, Bar Food, Restaurant Menu,
Accommodation, No Smoking Area,
Disabled Facilities

13 Bowd Inn

Bowd, Sidmouth, Devon EX10 0ND
Tel: 01395 513328

Real Ales, Bar Food, Restaurant Menu,
No Smoking Area, Disabled Facilities

14 The Cannon Inn

High St, Newton Poppleford, Sidmouth,
Devon EX10 0DW
Tel: 01395 568266

Real Ales, Restaurant Menu, Accommodation,
No Smoking Area, Disabled Facilities

See panel adjacent

15 The Carlton Inn

40-42 High St, Honiton, Devon EX14 1PJ
Tel: 01404 42903

Real Ales, Bar Food, Restaurant Menu,
No Smoking Area, Disabled Facilities

See panel on page 126

14 The Cannon Inn

Newton Poppleford, nr Sidmouth,
Devon EX10 0DW

☎ 01395 568266   🌐 www.cannoninn.co.uk

**Real Ales, Restaurant Menu, Accommodation,
No Smoking Area, Disabled Facilities**

☛	Off the main A3052 2 miles W of Sidford
🍺	Otter, Bass, Courage
🍴	12-2 & 6-9 (Sun to 7)
🛏	5 rooms
♫	Music Sun evening
🪑	Beer garden, car park
💳	Major cards accepted
🕐	11-3 & 5-11
🏛	Bicton Park 2 miles, Sidmouth 3 miles, Otterton Mill 3 miles, Budleigh Salterton 5 miles

The **Cannon Inn** is a handsome roadside hostelry in a village close to Sidmouth. It's a great place to stop for a drink and a snack in the bar or the garden, or to relax over a meal. The food choice runs from sandwiches and ploughman's platters to classic main courses such as battered cod, lasagne or chargrilled steaks. The inn also has 5 guest bedrooms.

16 Castle Inn

Castle Hill, Axminster, Devon EX13 5NN
Tel: 01297 34944

Real Ales, Bar Food, Restaurant Menu,
No Smoking Area, Disabled Facilities

17 The Catherine Wheel

Hemyock, Cullompton, Devon EX15 3RQ
Tel: 01823 680224

Real Ales, Bar Food, Restaurant Menu,
No Smoking Area, Disabled Facilities

18 Coffee & Lace

39 Harbour Rd, Seaton, Devon EX12 2LX
Tel: 01297 24145

Real Ales, Bar Food, Disabled Facilities

15 The Carlton Inn

High Street, Honiton, Devon EX14 1PJ

☎ 01404 42903

**Real Ales, Bar Food, Restaurant Menu,
No Smoking Area, Disabled Facilities**

☛ On the main street of Honiton, minutes from the A30 and A35

🍺 Courage, Fosters, John Smiths, Kronenborg, Grolsh, Guinness.

🍴 12-9

🎵 Night club every night

⛱ Beer garden, car park

💳 Major cards accepted

🕐 11-midnight (Wed to 1 am, Thurs to 2 am, Fri & Sat to 3 am, Sun to 1 am)

🏛 Museum and art galley in Honiton; Dumpton Hill 2 miles, Dunkeswell (Abbey and Memorial Museum) 5 miles

On the main street of Honiton, just moments from the A30 and A35, the **Carlton Inn** is a convivial old pub with a wide appeal. Stylishly decorated and furnished, it combines traditional and more contemporary elements, and the bar is a pleasant spot for enjoying good conversation and a glass or two at any time of day. Hot and cold snacks and meals are served from noon to 9 o'clock every day. In addition to fulfilling in fine style its role as a cheerful town pub, the Carlton has a surprise up its sleeve – an upstairs night club that's open till midnight or later every day of the week.

---

19 Colcombe Castle
Market Place, Colyton, Devon EX24 6JS
Tel: 01297 552257

Real Ales

20 Culm Valley Inn
Culmstock, Cullompton, Devon EX15 3JJ
Tel: 01884 840354

Real Ales, Bar Food, Restaurant Menu, Accommodation, No Smoking Area, Disabled Facilities

21 The Dog & Donkey
24 Knowle Village, Knowle, Budleigh Salterton, Devon EX9 6AL
Tel: 01395 442021

Real Ales, Bar Food, Restaurant Menu

22 Dolphin Hotel
Fore St, Beer, Seaton, Devon EX12 3EQ
Tel: 01297 20068

Real Ales, Bar Food, Restaurant Menu, Accommodation, No Smoking Area

23 Drewe Arms
Broadhembury, Devon EX14 0NF
Tel: 01404 841267

Real Ales, Bar Food, Restaurant Menu, Accommodation, No Smoking Area, Disabled Facilities

24 Dukes
Market Place, Sidmouth, Devon EX10 8AR
Tel: 01395 513320

Real Ales, Bar Food, Restaurant Menu, Accommodation, No Smoking Area, Disabled Facilities

25 The Exeter Inn
High St, Newton Poppleford, Sidmouth, Devon EX10 0EG
Tel: 01395 568295

Real Ales, Bar Food, No Smoking Area, Disabled Facilities

26 The Famous George Inn

The Square, Seaton, Devon EX12 2NX
Tel: 01297 625506

Real Ales, Bar Food, Restaurant Menu, No Smoking
Area, Disabled Facilities

27 **The Feathers**

35 High St, Budleigh Salterton, Devon EX9 6LE
Tel: 01395 442042

Real Ales, Bar Food

See panel below

28 Fishponds House Hotel

Dunkeswell, Honiton, Devon EX14 4SH
Tel: 01404 891287

Real Ales, Bar Food, Restaurant Menu,
Accommodation, No Smoking Area,
Disabled Facilities

29 The Flintlock Inn

Marsh, Honiton, Devon EX14 9AJ
Tel: 01460 234403

Real Ales, Bar Food, Restaurant Menu,
No Smoking Area, Disabled Facilities

30 Fortfield Hotel

Fortfield Place, Sidmouth, Devon EX10 8NU
Tel: 01395 512403

Bar Food, Restaurant Menu, Accommodation,
No Smoking Area, Disabled Facilities

31 The Fountain Head

Branscombe, Seaton, Devon EX12 3BG
Tel: 01297 680359

Real Ales, Bar Food, Restaurant Menu,
No Smoking Area, Disabled Facilities

---

27 **The Feathers**

35 High Street, Budleigh Salterton, Devon EX9 6LE
☎ 01395 442042

Real Ales, Bar Food

 On the main street of Budleigh Salterton, 5
miles SW of Sidmouth on the B3178

 Branoc, Wadworth, Bass & Guest

 12-2.15 & 6-8.15

 Quiz Sunday

 Beer garden, patio

 11-11

🏛 Bicton Park Botanical Gardens 2 miles,
Sidmouth 5 miles

The Prince of Wales feathers grace the sign
outside this fine old former coaching inn
on a corner site in the heart of Budleigh
Salterton. Behind its attractive façade, the
Feathers has a very comfortable open-plan
bar that stretches all the way back to a
secluded beer garden. Four cask ales are
always on tap, to enjoy over a chat with friends
or local customers, or to complement a meal.
Food is king at John and Joan Salt's outstanding
pub, with locally caught fish among the
favourite dishes. The menus take their
inspiration from far and wide, and on a busy
day they serve over 100 meals, proof indeed
that this is one of the most popular eating
places in the region. Food is available every
session except Sunday evening, when the
weekly quiz provides ample food for thought.

33 The George Inn

Chard Street, Chardstock, nr Axminster,
Devon EX13 7BX

☎ 01460 220241 🌐 www.george-inn.co.uk

Real Ales, Bar Food, Restaurant Menu,
Accommodation, No Smoking Area, Disabled
Facilities

- 🖝 Chardstock lies off the A358 between Chard and Axminster
- ∥ 12-2 & 7-9
- ⊨ 4 en suite rooms
- ⚒ Courtyard garden, car park
- 💳 Major cards accepted
- ⏰ 12-2.30 & 6-11 (Sat all day, Sun 12-3 & 7-10.30)
- 🏛 Chard 3 miles, Forde Abbey 4 miles, Axminster 5 miles

Owners Adam Snow and Varry Taylor and their excellent staff combine to make the **George Inn** one of the very best

hostelries in the region. In the centre of picturesque Chardstock, the building was originally the Church House, where churchgoers would gather after the service to sample the beer brewed by the church warden. Thus the long tradition of hospitality began, and when it became a public house some of the regulars liked the place so much that they stayed behind when they departed this life – the inn has several ghosts, but they're all much too polite to disturb today's visitors. Others have left behind a more tangible legacy, and the initials carved into the ancient stone window surrounds can be traced back through many generations of local families.

The George boasts many original features, including old oak and linenfold panelling. The panelling in the lounge is particularly fine, and graced a ship's cabin and a church before being installed here. In one corner visitors can read the works of the inn's resident poet Arthur Lord that chronicle events if the pub and village over the last 20 years. On winter nights there's no better place to be than chatting with the locals by the fire over a glass of ale, but this is definitely a place for all seasons, summer evenings can pass perfectly under the fairy lights in the courtyard.

The food served at the George is prepared by Adam and his team from the finest local produce for a menu that varies from old favourites such as beer-battered cod or steak & kidney pie to fish specials, seasonal game and signature gourmet dishes like slow-roast half-shoulder of lamb with honey and rosemary or pan-fried breast of chicken with a creamy tarragon and sherry sauce. Booking is advisable, particularly on Saturday nights.

The George is definitely a place to tarry, and guests will find character and comfort in four cottage-style bedrooms at the rear of the pub.

32 ## The George Hotel

George St, Axminster, Devon EX13 5DW
Tel: 01297 32209

Real Ales, Bar Food, Restaurant Menu,
Accommodation, No Smoking Area,
Disabled Facilities

33 ## The George Inn

Chardstock, Axminster, Devon EX13 7BX
Tel: 01460 220241

Real Ales, Bar Food, Restaurant Menu,
Accommodation, No Smoking Area,
Disabled Facilities

See panel opposite

34 ## The George Inn

Commercial Rd, Uffculme, Cullompton,
Devon EX15 3EB
Tel: 01884 841903

Real Ales, Bar Food, Restaurant Menu,
No Smoking Area, Disabled Facilities

35 ## Gerrard Arms

Rosemary Lane, Colyton, Devon EX24 6LN
Tel: 01297 552588

Real Ales, Bar Food

36 ## The Golden Hind

The Street, Musbury, Axminster,
Devon EX13 8AU
Tel: 01297 552413

Real Ales, Bar Food

37 ## The Golden Lion

Tipton St. John, Sidmouth, Devon EX10 0AA
Tel: 01404 812881

Real Ales, Bar Food, Restaurant Menu,
Accommodation, No Smoking Area,
Disabled Facilities

38 ## The Greyhound Inn & Hotel

Fenny Bridges, Honiton, Devon EX14 3BJ
Tel: 01404 850380

Real Ales, Bar Food, Restaurant Menu,
Accommodation, No Smoking Area

39 ## Half Moon Inn

Half Moon Inn, Clayhidon, Cullompton,
Devon EX15 3TJ
Tel: 01823 680291

Real Ales, Bar Food, Restaurant Menu,
No Smoking Area

40 ## Harbour Inn

Church St, Axmouth, Seaton, Devon EX12 4AF
Tel: 01297 20371

Real Ales, Bar Food, Restaurant Menu,
No Smoking Area, Disabled Facilities

41 ## Hare & Hounds

Putts Corner, Sidbury, Sidmouth,
Devon EX10 0QQ
Tel: 01404 41760

Real Ales, Bar Food, Restaurant Menu,
No Smoking Area

42 ## The Heathfield Inn

Walnut Rd, Honiton, Devon EX14 2UG
Tel: 01404 45321

Real Ales, Bar Food, Restaurant Menu,
Accommodation, No Smoking Area,
Disabled Facilities

43 ## Home Farm Hotel

Wilmington, Honiton, Devon EX14 9JR
Tel: 01404 831278

Bar Food, Restaurant Menu, Accommodation,
No Smoking Area, Disabled Facilities

44 ## Honiton Motel

Exeter Rd, Honiton, Devon EX14 1BL
Tel: 01404 43440

Bar Food, Restaurant Menu, Accommodation,
No Smoking Area, Disabled Facilities

45 ## Honiton Wine Bar

High St, Honiton, Devon EX14 1PG
Tel: 01404 47889

Real Ales, Bar Food, Restaurant Menu,
No Smoking Area, Disabled Facilities

46 The Hook & Parrot
East Walk, Seaton, Devon EX12 2LN
Tel: 01297 20222

Real Ales, Bar Food, Restaurant Menu,
No Smoking Area, Disabled Facilities

47 Hotel Riviera
The Esplanade, Sidmouth, Devon EX10 8AY
Tel: 01395 515201

Bar Food, Restaurant Menu, Accommodation,
No Smoking Area, Disabled Facilities

48 Hunters Lodge Inn
Charmouth Rd, Axminster, Devon EX13 5SZ
Tel: 01297 33286

Real Ales, Bar Food, Restaurant Menu,
No Smoking Area, Disabled Facilities

49 Keepers Cottage Inn
Kentisbeare, Cullompton, Devon EX15 2EB
Tel: 01884 266247

Real Ales, Bar Food, Restaurant Menu,
No Smoking Area, Disabled Facilities

50 King William Hotel
7 High St, Budleigh Salterton, Devon EX9 6LD
Tel: 01395 442075

No Smoking Area, Disabled Facilities

51 52 The Kingfisher
Dolphin St, Colyton, Devon EX24 6NA
Tel: 01297 552476

Real Ales, Bar Food, Restaurant Menu,
No Smoking Area

53 The Kings Arms Otterton
Fore Street, Otterton, Devon EX9 7HB

☎ 01395 568416

🌐 www.kingsarmsottertondevon.co.uk
e-mail: info@kingsarmsotterton.co.uk

**Real Ales, Bar Food, Restaurant Menu,
Accommodation, No Smoking Area,
Disabled Facilities**

☛ Off the B3178 3 miles SW of Sidmouth

🍺 Otter, Spitfire

🍴 12-9.30

🛏 9 en suite rooms

🎵 Quiz 2nd Sunday of the month

🏕 Beer garden, car park

💳 Major cards accepted

🕐 open all day

🏛 Otterton Mill & Museum 1 mile, Bicton Park 2 miles, Budleigh Salterton 2 miles, Sidmouth 3 miles

The Kings Arms Otterton is a pretty and traditional country pub set in the picturesque village of Otterton in East Devon.

Close to local beaches with beautiful riverside and country walks.

Family and dog friendly with a large beer garden and ample parking.

Open all day, they offer you a superb choice of freshly cooked dishes using high quality local produce wherever possible, complimented by fine wines and a broad selection of well kept real ales and beers.

The Hotel has en-suite rooms at affordable rates for everyone, from single occupancy to families with dogs. Please see website for more details.

52 The Kings Arms

Gold St, Ottery St. Mary, Devon EX11 1DG
Tel: 01404 812486

Real Ales

53 The Kings Arms

Fore St, Otterton, Budleigh Salterton,
Devon EX9 7HB
Tel: 01395 568416

Real Ales, Bar Food, Restaurant Menu,
Accommodation, No Smoking Area,
Disabled Facilities

See panel opposite

54 The Kings Arms

Fore St, Seaton, Devon EX12 2AN
Tel: 01297 23431

Real Ales, Bar Food, Restaurant Menu,
No Smoking Area, Disabled Facilities

55 The Kings Arms Inn

Stockland, Honiton, Devon EX14 9BS
Tel: 01404 881361

Real Ales, Bar Food, Restaurant Menu,
Accommodation, No Smoking Area

56 The Lamb & Flag

Batts Lane, Ottery St. Mary, Devon EX11 1EY
Tel: 01404 812616

Real Ales, Disabled Facilities

57 The Lamb Inn

Lyme Rd, Axminster, Devon EX13 5BE
Tel: 01297 33922

Real Ales, Disabled Facilities

58 The London Inn

Gold St, Ottery St. Mary, Devon EX11 1DG
Tel: 01404 814763

Real Ales, Bar Food, Restaurant Menu,
Accommodation, No Smoking Area,
Disabled Facilities

See panel adjacent

58 The London Inn

Gold Street, Ottery St Mary, Devon EX11 1DG
☎ 01404 814763

**Real Ales, Bar Food, Restaurant Menu,
Accommodation, No Smoking Area,
Disabled Facilities**

☞ In the centre of Ottery St Mary, on the B3177, off the A30 5 miles SW of Honiton

🍺 Adnams, Old Speckled Hen

🍴 12-2 & 7-9; simple snacks all day

🛏 4 en suite rooms

🚗 Car park

💳 Major cards accepted

🕐 11.30-3 & 6-11 (sat & Sun all day)

🏛 Cadhay Manor House 1 mile, Honiton 5 miles, Sidmouth 7 miles, Exeter 10 miles

You will receive a warm welcome at the London Inn. There is an American flavour to some of the dishes on the wide-ranging menu, while others are classics such as spaghetti Bolognese or treacle sponge pudding. The inn has 4 en suite rooms for B&B guests.

59 The Marine

The Esplanade, Sidmouth, Devon EX10 8BB
Tel: 01395 513145

Real Ales, Bar Food, Disabled Facilities

61 The Merry Harriers

Forches Corner, Clayhidon, Devon EX15 3TR

☎ 01823 421270 ⊕ www.merryharriers.co.uk

Real Ales, Bar Food, Restaurant Menu, No Smoking Area, Disabled Facilities

- 🚩 Off the A38 at Taunton or Wellington, or off the M5 (J26)
- 🍺 Selection from West Country breweries
- 🍴 12-2.30 & 6.30-9
- 🛏 4 rooms to open in 2006
- ⚓ Garden, car park
- 💳 Major cards accepted
- 🕐 12-3 & 6.30-11 (closed Sunday eve and all day Monday except Bank Holidays)
- 🏛 Blackdown Hills 1 mile, Wellington 5 miles, Taunton 8 miles

A short detour from the M5 (J26) or a pleasant drive from Taunton or Wellington brings visitors to the **Merry Harriers**. This characterful country pub, which actually lies just across the county border into Somerset,

It's a great place for a drink, with a fine selection of local beers and ciders and an excellent choice of wines to enjoy in the beamed bars with cosy nooks. It's also a place well worth seeking out for a meal, and in the several well-appointed eating areas fresh produce is put to excellent use on the wide-ranging menus. Brixham scallops and sole are always popular, and other typical temptations include pork & venison pâté with rowanberry jelly, king prawns in filo pastry and Blackdown duck confit served on a bed of onion marmalade. Vegetarians are well catered for with imaginative options such as sweet potato and cashew nut korma.

Having established the Merry Harriers as a super 'local' and destination restaurant, Peter intends to make this outstanding inn a great place to stay by converting the skittle alley into four letting rooms due to come on stream by early 2006. The inn stands on the once notorious Forches Corner, where the records show that ambushes took place during the 17th century Monmouth Rebellion and in the 18th century. Some of the highwaymen caught were hanged here, which could account for the inn's resident ghost being a headless horseman! This is great walking country, with the Blackdown Hills nearby and no fear of being made to stand and deliver.

has go-ahead hosts in Peter and Angela Gatling. Peter is the meeter and greeter, and with Angela and some of the friendliest staff you'll ever meet he intends to make this already popular pub known to an even wider clientele.

60 The Masons Arms

Branscombe, Seaton, Devon EX12 3DJ
Tel: 01297 680300

Real Ales, Bar Food, Restaurant Menu,
Accommodation, No Smoking Area

61 **The Merry Harriers**

Clayhidon, Cullompton, Devon EX15 3PT
Tel: 01823 421270

Real Ales, Bar Food, Restaurant Menu,
No Smoking Area, Disabled Facilities

See panel opposite

62 Monkton Court Hotel

Monkton, Honiton, Devon EX14 9QH
Tel: 01404 42309

Bar Food, Restaurant Menu, Accommodation,
No Smoking Area, Disabled Facilities

63 The New Dolphin Hotel

115 High St, Honiton, Devon EX14 1LS
Tel: 01404 42377

Bar Food, Restaurant Menu, Accommodation,
No Smoking Area, Disabled Facilities

64 The New Inn

The Hill, Kilmington, Axminster, Devon EX13 7SF
Tel: 01297 33376

Real Ales, Restaurant Menu, No Smoking Area

65 Nog Inn

Feniton, Honiton, Devon EX14 3BT
Tel: 01404 850210

Real Ales

66 The Old Inn

Hawkchurch, Axminster, Devon EX13 5XD
Tel: 01297 678309

Real Ales, Bar Food, Restaurant Menu,
No Smoking Area, Disabled Facilities

67 The Old Inn

Kilmington, Axminster, Devon EX13 7RB
Tel: 01297 32096

Real Ales, Bar Food, Restaurant Menu,
No Smoking Area, Disabled Facilities

68 Old Ship Inn

Old Fore St, Sidmouth, Devon EX10 8LP
Tel: 01395 512127

Real Ales, Bar Food, Restaurant Menu,
No Smoking Area, Disabled Facilities

69 Ostler Inn

Commercial Rd, Uffculme, Cullompton,
Devon EX15 3EB
Tel: 01884 840260

Real Ales, Bar Food, No Smoking Area,
Disabled Facilities

70 The Otter Inn

Exmouth Rd, Colaton Raleigh, Sidmouth,
Devon EX10 0LE
Tel: 01395 568434

Real Ales, Bar Food, Restaurant Menu,
No Smoking Area

71 The Otter Inn

Weston, Honiton, Devon EX14 3NZ
Tel: 01404 42594

Real Ales, Bar Food, Restaurant Menu,
No Smoking Area, Disabled Facilities

72 Ottery Indian Cuisine & Hotel

5 Cornhill Court, Ottery St Mary,
Devon EX11 1DW
Tel: 01404 811088

Real Ales, Restaurant Menu, Accommodation,
No Smoking Area

73 Poachers Pocket

Redball, Burlescombe, Tiverton, Devon EX16 7JY
Tel: 01823 672286

Real Ales, Bar Food, Restaurant Menu,
Accommodation, No Smoking Area,
Disabled Facilities

74 Radway Inn

1 Radway Place, Sidmouth, Devon EX10 8PY
Tel: 01395 578305

Real Ales, No Smoking Area, Disabled Facilities

75 The Railway Inn

Queen St, Honiton, Devon EX14 1HE
Tel: 01404 43686

Real Ales

76 The Red Cow Inn

43 High St, Honiton, Devon EX14 1PW
Tel: 01404 47497

Real Ales, Bar Food, Restaurant Menu

77 The Red Lion Inn

Fore St, Sidbury, Sidmouth, Devon EX10 0SD
Tel: 01395 597313

Real Ales, Bar Food, Restaurant Menu,
Accommodation, No Smoking Area

78 The Red Lion Inn

Lyme St, Axminster, Devon EX13 5AU
Tel: 01297 32016

Real Ales, Bar Food, Restaurant Menu,
No Smoking Area, Disabled Facilities

79 The Ridgeway Inn

Smallridge, Axminster, Devon EX13 7JJ
Tel: 01297 32171

Real Ales, Bar Food, Restaurant Menu,
No Smoking Area, Disabled Facilities

80 The Rising Sun

School St, Sidford, Sidmouth, Devon EX10 9PF
Tel: 01395 513722

Real Ales, Bar Food, Restaurant Menu,
No Smoking Area, Disabled Facilities

See panel adjacent

81 Rolle Arms

Lower Budleigh, East Budleigh, Budleigh Salterton,
Devon EX9 7DL
Tel: 01395 442012

Real Ales, Bar Food, Restaurant Menu,
No Smoking Area, Disabled Facilities

82 Royal Glen Hotel

Glen Rd, Sidmouth, Devon EX10 8RW
Tel: 01395 513221

Bar Food, Restaurant Menu, Accommodation,
No Smoking Area, Disabled Facilities

80 The Rising Sun

School Street, Sidford, nr Sidmouth,
Devon EX10 9PF
☎ 01395 513722

Real Ales, Bar Food, Restaurant Menu,
No Smoking Area, Disabled Facilities

☛ Sidford lies at the junction of the A375 from Honiton and the A3052 Seaton-Exeter road

🍺 4/5 changing ales

🍴 12-2 & 6.30-9 Tues-Sat, Sunday lunch 12-2

🅿 Car park

💳 Major cards accepted

🕐 11-3 & 6-11 (all day Sat & Sun)

🏛 Sidbury 1 mile, Sidmouth 1½ miles

Behind its long black-and-white frontage, the **Rising Sun** has a cosy bar where connoisseurs of real ales are in their element. The excellent selection is supplied mainly by local breweries, and the friendly Austin family also provide visitors with a good choice of unpretentious, well-priced pub dishes. Beautiful flower displays are a feature of this deservedly popular pub.

83 Royal Oak

Dunkeswell, Honiton, Devon EX14 4RE
Tel: 01404 891683

Real Ales, Bar Food, Restaurant Menu,
No Smoking Area, Disabled Facilities

84 Royal York & Faulkner Hotel

The Esplande, Sidmouth, Devon EX10 8AZ
Tel: 01395 513043

Bar Food, Restaurant Menu, Accommodation,
Disabled Facilities

85 Salston Manor Hotel

Fluxton Rd, Ottery St Mary, Exeter,
Devon EX11 1RQ
Tel: 01404 815581

Bar Food, Restaurant Menu, Accommodation,
No Smoking Area, Disabled Facilities

86 The Salty Monk

Church St, Sidford, Sidmouth, Devon EX10 9QP
Tel: 01395 513174

Restaurant Menu, Accommodation,
No Smoking Area

87 The Ship Inn

Church St, Axmouth, Seaton, Devon EX12 4AF
Tel: 01297 21838

Real Ales, Bar Food, Restaurant Menu,
No Smoking Area, Disabled Facilities

88 **The Sidmouth Arms**

Upottery, Honiton, Devon EX14 9PN
Tel: 01404 861252

Real Ales, Bar Food, Restaurant Menu,
Accommodation, No Smoking Area

See panel on page 136

89 Sir Walter Raleigh

22 High St, East Budleigh, Budleigh Salterton, Devon
EX9 7ED
Tel: 01395 442510

Real Ales, Bar Food, Restaurant Menu,
No Smoking Area, Disabled Facilities

90 Six Bells Inn

Payhembury, Honiton, Devon EX14 3HR
Tel: 01404 841261

Real Ales, Bar Food, Restaurant Menu,
No Smoking Area, Disabled Facilities

91 The Star Inn

New St, Honiton, Devon EX14 1BS
Tel: 01404 42045

Real Ales

92 The Swan Inn

37 York St, Sidmouth, Devon EX10 8BY
Tel: 01395 512849

Real Ales, Bar Food, Restaurant Menu,
No Smoking Area, Disabled Facilities

93 The Talaton Inn

Talaton, Exeter, Devon EX5 2RQ
Tel: 01404 822214

Real Ales, Bar Food, Restaurant Menu,
No Smoking Area, Disabled Facilities

94 Time

Old Fore St, Market Square, Sidmouth,
Devon EX10 8LS
Tel: 01395 579449

Restaurant Menu, No Smoking Area,
Disabled Facilities

95 The Tuckers Arms

Dalwood, Devon EX13 7EG
Tel: 01404 881342

Real Ales, Bar Food, Restaurant Menu,
No Smoking Area, Disabled Facilities

96 Tudor Rose

High St, Sidmouth, Devon EX10 8EL
Tel: 01395 514720

Real Ales, Bar Food, Restaurant Menu,
No Smoking Area

97 Tytherleigh Arms

Tytherleigh, Axminster, Devon EX13 7BE
Tel: 01460 220214

Real Ales, Bar Food, Restaurant Menu,
Accommodation, No Smoking Area,
Disabled Facilities

98 The Vault Bar

Bank House, Marine Place, Seaton,
Devon EX12 2LL
Tel: 01297 625333

Real Ales, Bar Food, No Smoking Area

99 Victoria Hotel

The Esplanade, Sidmouth, Devon EX10 8RY
Tel: 01395 512651

Bar Food, Restaurant Menu, Accommodation,
No Smoking Area, Disabled Facilities

88 The Sidmouth Arms

Upottery, nr Honiton, Devon EX14 9PN

 01404 861252   www.thesidmoutharms.co.uk

**Real Ales, Bar Food, Restaurant Menu,
Accommodation, No Smoking Area**

- The inn stands by the church in Upottery, off the A30 between Chard and Honiton
- Otter, Bass
- 12-2 & 6-9
- 3 rooms
- Skittle alley, pool
- Patio, car park
- Major cards accepted
- 11.30-2.30 & 6-11 (Sun 7-10.30)
- Stockland Hill Earthworks 2 miles, Honiton 6 miles, Chard 8 miles

Standing close to the church in the picture-postcard village of Upottery, the **Sidmouth Arms** has a popular, hardworking leaseholder in Mike Spiller, who runs the inn with his son

Ross and Linda the cook. Just off the A30 between Chard and Honiton, it dates back over 300 years, and was originally called the George; it changed its name when the village and the estate became the property of Lord Sidmouth.

Mike, who was born and raised in Upottery, has made many friends since taking over the lease in 2001, and both the locals and the visitors to this pleasant part of the world are equally appreciative of the warm welcome and the friendly, relaxed ambience, the well-kept

real ales and Linda's super cooking. The pub retains abundant old-world charm both in its pretty stone frontage and in the bar and dining areas, and the beer garden is a top spot in summer, with the added attraction of an aviary. Linda's classic dishes, including cottage pie, steaks and the Sunday roasts, are popular choices, but many diners look to the artistically decorated blackboard of fish specials typified by grilled whole sea bass and baked trout or salmon. Much of the fish landed by local boats, and the meat is also locally sourced as far as possible.

The inn has three comfortably appointed guest bedrooms that are available all year round, providing a friendly, civilised base for exploring the region. This is great walking country, and for motorists the towns of Honiton and Chard are an easy drive away. Also nearby, in the heart of the Blackdown Plateau, is the little village of Dunkeswell, where the Church of St Nicholas and the Memorial Museum dedicated to RAF and USAAF personnel who served at the base are both well worth a visit.

100 Vine Inn

Vine Passage, Honiton, Devon EX14 1NN
Tel: 01404 42889

Real Ales, Bar Food, No Smoking Area

101 The Volunteer

177 High St, Honiton, Devon EX14 1LQ
Tel: 01404 42145

Real Ales, Bar Food, Restaurant Menu,
No Smoking Area, Disabled Facilities

102 The Volunteer Inn

52 Temple St, Sidmouth, Devon EX10 9BQ
Tel: 01395 512498

Real Ales, Bar Food, Restaurant Menu,
No Smoking Area

103 The Volunteer Inn

1 Broad St, Ottery St. Mary, Devon EX11 1BZ
Tel: 01404 812445

Real Ales, Bar Food, Restaurant Menu,
No Smoking Area, Disabled Facilities

104 The Waterloo Cross Inn

Uffculme, Cullompton, Devon EX15 3ES
Tel: 01884 840328

Real Ales, Bar Food, Restaurant Menu,
No Smoking Area, Disabled Facilities

105 Westcliff Hotel

Manor Rd, Sidmouth, Devon EX10 8RU
Tel: 01395 513252

Bar Food, Restaurant Menu, Accommodation,
No Smoking Area, Disabled Facilities

106 Wheelwright Inn

Swan Hill Rd Colyford, Colyton,
Devon EX24 6QQ
Tel: 01297 552585

Real Ales, Bar Food, Restaurant Menu,
No Smoking Area, Disabled Facilities

107 The White Hart Inn

Wilmington, Honiton, Devon EX14 9JQ
Tel: 01404 831764

Real Ales, Bar Food, Restaurant Menu,
Accommodation, No Smoking Area

110 Woodlands Hotel

Station Road, Sidmouth, Devon EX10 8HG

☎ 01395 513120 🌐 www.woodlands-hotel.com

**Bar Food, Restaurant Menu, Accommodation,
No Smoking Area, Disabled Facilities**

- In Sidmouth 400 yards up from the beach
- Otter
- All day
- 20 en suite rooms
- Garden, car park
- Major cards accepted
- All day
- Beach 400 yards, Donkey Sanctuary 2 miles, Old Bakery NT 3 miles

Woodlands Hotel is a short walk from the esplanade and beach. Twenty individually styled rooms offer comfortable accommodation. Fresh local produce and locally caught fish are used whenever possible. Morning coffee, lunches and afternoon teas are served in the bar, lounge and garden.

| | | Wyndham Arms

Kentisbeare, nr Cullompton, Devon EX15 2AA

☎ 01884 266327

**Real Ales, Bar Food, Restaurant Menu,
No Smoking Area, Disabled Facilities**

☞ From Cullompton or J28 of the M5 take the A373; turn left to Kentisbeare after about 2 miles

🍺 Otter + guests

🍴 Lunchtime and evening

⛺ Garden, car park

💳 Major cards accepted

🕐 12-11

🏛 Cullompton 3 miles

On a site occupied since the 13th century, the long frontage of the **Wyndham Arms** dominated the centre of the little hamlet of Kentisbeare, 3 miles from Cullompton on the Honiton road. Ancient beams and floors, whitewashed walls and a variety of chairs and tables create a delightfully rustic, old-world look in the bar, and the courtyard beer garden offers a pleasant alternative when the sun shines. Otter is the resident cask ale, and a selection of wines is available by glass (175 or 250cl) or bottle. Good home-cooked food is served lunchtime and evening, typified by chicken Caesar salad, minted lamb shank, tuna steak with lemon butter and steak & Otter ale pie. A separate board lists desserts including a fine range of ice creams.

108 White Hart Inn

Swan Hill Rd, Colyford, Colyton,
Devon EX24 6QF
Tel: 01297 553201

Real Ales, Bar Food, Restaurant Menu,
No Smoking Area, Disabled Facilities

109 Winstons

Beach Rd, Seaton, Devon EX12 2LZ
Tel: 01297 20494

Real Ales, Bar Food, Restaurant Menu,
No Smoking Area, Disabled Facilities

110 Woodlands Hotel

Station Rd, Sidmouth, Devon EX10 8HG
Tel: 01395 513774

Bar Food, Restaurant Menu, Accommodation,
No Smoking Area, Disabled Facilities

See panel on page 137

| | | Wyndham Arms Inn

High St, Kentisbeare, Cullompton,
Devon EX15 2AA
Tel: 01884 266327

Real Ales, Bar Food, Restaurant Menu,
No Smoking Area, Disabled Facilities

See panel above

112 Yarcombe Inn

Yarcombe, Honiton, Devon EX14 9BD
Tel: 01404 861676

Real Ales, Bar Food, Restaurant Menu,
Accommodation, No Smoking Area,
Disabled Facilities

TRAVEL PUBLISHING ORDER FORM

To order any of our publications just fill in the payment details below and complete the order form.
For orders of less than 4 copies please add £1 per book for postage and packing.
Orders over 4 copies are P & P free.

Please Complete Either:

I enclose a cheque for £ [＿＿＿＿＿] made payable to *Travel Publishing Ltd*

Or:

Card No: [＿＿＿＿＿＿＿＿＿]   Expiry Date: [＿＿＿＿＿]

Signature: [＿＿＿＿＿＿＿＿＿]

Name: [＿＿＿＿＿＿＿＿＿]

Address: [＿＿＿＿＿＿＿＿＿]

Tel no: [＿＿＿＿＿＿＿＿＿]

Please either send, telephone, fax or e-mail your order to:
Travel Publishing Ltd, 7a Apollo House, Calleva Park, Aldermaston, Berkshire RG7 8TN
Tel: **0118 981 7777**   Fax: **0118 982 0077**   e-mail: **info@travelpublishing.co.uk**

	Price	Quantity
HIDDEN PLACES REGIONAL TITLES		
Cornwall	£8.99	....
Devon	£8.99	....
Dorset, Hants & Isle of Wight	£8.99	....
East Anglia	£8.99	....
Lake District & Cumbria	£8.99	....
Northumberland & Durham	£8.99	....
Peak District	£8.99	....
Sussex	£8.99	....
Yorkshire	£8.99	....
HIDDEN PLACES NATIONAL TITLES		
England	£11.99	....
Ireland	£11.99	....
Scotland	£11.99	....
Wales	£11.99	....
HIDDEN INNS TITLES		
East Anglia	£7.99	....
Heart of England	£7.99	....
North of England	£7.99	....
South	£7.99	....
South East	£7.99	....
Wales	£7.99	....
West Country	£7.99	....
Yorkshire	£7.99	....

	Price	Quantity
COUNTRY PUBS AND INNS		
Cornwall	£5.99	....
Devon	£7.99	....
Sussex	£7.99	....
Wales	£8.99	....
COUNTRY LIVING RURAL GUIDES		
East Anglia	£10.99	....
Heart of England	£10.99	....
Ireland	£11.99	....
North East	£10.99	....
North West	£10.99	....
Scotland	£11.99	....
South of England	£10.99	....
South East of England	£10.99	....
Wales	£11.99	....
West Country	£10.99	....
OTHER TITLES		
Off the Motorway	£11.99	....

Total Quantity: [＿＿＿＿＿]

Post & Packing: [＿＿＿＿＿]

Total Value: [＿＿＿＿＿]

Reader Reaction Form

The *Travel Publishing* research team would like to receive reader's comments on any pubs and inns covered (or not covered) in this guide so please do not hesitate to write to us using these reader reaction forms. We would also welcome recommendations for suitable entries to be included in the next edition. This will help ensure that the *Country Pubs and Inns series of Guides* continues to provide a comprehensive list of pubs and inns to our readers. To provide your comments or recommendations would you please complete the forms below and overleaf as indicated and send to:

**The Research Department, Travel Publishing Ltd,
7a Apollo House, Calleva Park, Aldermaston, Reading, RG7 8TN.**

Your Name:

Your Address:

Your Telephone Number:

Please tick as appropriate:

Comments ☐   Recommendation ☐

Name of Establishment:

Address:

Telephone Number:

Name of Contact:

Reader Reaction Form

Comment or Reason for Recommendation:

....

....

....

....

....

....

....

....

....

....

....

....

....

....

....

....

....

Reader Reaction Form

The *Travel Publishing* research team would like to receive reader's comments on any pubs and inns covered (or not covered) in this guide so please do not hesitate to write to us using these reader reaction forms. We would also welcome recommendations for suitable entries to be included in the next edition. This will help ensure that the *Country Pubs and Inns series of Guides* continues to provide a comprehensive list of pubs and inns to our readers. To provide your comments or recommendations would you please complete the forms below and overleaf as indicated and send to:

The Research Department, Travel Publishing Ltd,
7a Apollo House, Calleva Park, Aldermaston, Reading, RG7 8TN.

Your Name:

Your Address:

Your Telephone Number:

Please tick as appropriate:

Comments ☐   Recommendation ☐

Name of Establishment:

Address:

Telephone Number:

Name of Contact:

Reader Reaction Form

Comment or Reason for Recommendation:

....

....

....

....

....

....

....

....

....

....

....

....

....

....

....

....

....

....